MW01295932

Highly Sensitive Empaths and Narcissistic Abuse

The Complete Survival Guide to Understanding Your Gift, the Toxic Relationship to Narcissists and Energy Vampires, and How to Protect, Heal and Recover

J. Vandeweghe

Table of Contents

FREE AUDIOBOOK

Feel like listening instead?

Save yourself $19.95 and click the link below to get the Audiobook Edition for FREE

For US:

For UK:

Please note: Must be a new member to Audible

Highly Sensitive Empaths

The Complete Survival Guide to Self-Discovery, Protection from Narcissists and Energy Vampires, and Developing the Empath Gift.

J. Vandeweghe

Free E-book and Newsletter

6 WAYS TO THRIVE AS AN EMPATH AND LIVE A GREAT LIFE

Click the link below to sign up to the newsletter and receive your free eBook on 6 Ways to Thrive as an Empath and Live a Great Life. I promise, there's a ton of value in it!

http://bit.ly/Thriving-As-An-Empath

Introduction

Thank you for purchasing *"Highly Sensitive Empaths: The Complete Survival Guide to Self-Discovery, Protection from Narcissists and Energy Vampires, and Developing the Empath Gift."*

By purchasing this book, I am assuming you either: a) know you are an Empath, or b) are curious about whether you are an Empath. Either way, this book is the perfect read for you. This book is designed to give you a stronger understanding on what it means to be an Empath, how it has likely impacted you throughout your life, and how you can protect yourself and care for yourself so that you can nurture and master this incredible gift.

Since there is a chance that you may be reading this book wondering if you are in fact an Empath or not, I wanted to start out by including a basic checklist to help you decide "yes or no." If you determine yes, then you know this book is exactly what you have been looking for.

Here is your basic checklist. Mark off any statement that accurately reflects you. You will find a more in-depth checklist in Chapter 1.

- "I am prone to experiencing bouts of anxiety and depression."
- "Crowded places tend to make me feel overwhelmed."
- "I am passionate about helping other people."
- "As a child, I was sensitive to the emotions of others. Especially figures of authority."
- "I often feel drained after hanging out with certain people for too long."
- "My mood seems to change for no reason."
- "I can often feel what others are feeling as though it is happening to me personally."
- "I tend to be introverted, even though I may like spending time with other people."
- "Solitude is where I feel most connected and clear so that I can enjoy myself."

- "My nerves can be overwhelmed from hearing too many sounds or smell to many smells."
- "I have a hard time falling asleep, sometimes I even procrastinate going to bed."
- "Sometimes I can feel the presence of beings who are not actually there."
- "Bright lights and bad smells can shift my mood and make me deeply uncomfortable."
- "I have a deep love for nature."

These bullet points are to give you a basic understanding of what Empaths can experience. If you are still not 100% sure yet, do not worry, we will be taking a deeper look into the Empath traits in the next chapter. Throughout the pages in this book, you are going to learn about what it means to be an Empath and how you can properly care for yourself as one. This will allow you to reclaim your quality of life and begin to experience things that may have previously been too overwhelming for you.

Know that you are not alone in being an Empath, and being one is a highly treasured gift that allows you to bring great value to the world. As you read more, you will grow to understand what this all means and how you can build your gift to begin having a massive impact on the betterment of society, without draining yourself or giving yourself away in favor of this mission.

Enjoy.

Chapter 1: Is This You?

"The only true happiness lies in knowing who you are."
- *Laurell K. Hamilton*

For many people, discovering a new label for how you identify and who you are can be both scary and liberating. On one hand, you have a new term for who and what you are. This means that you are now "diagnosed" as a certain type of person. However, it also means that you are now able to discover more about yourself. Having a label for who and what you are opens up the opportunity to learn what that means and how it impacts you in your life. As a result, it can be liberating to know that you are not alone and that there are ways for you to create a powerful and enjoyable life with your new label in tow.

Like all other labels, identifying as an Empath is not entirely by choice. Rather, you either are an Empath, or you aren't one. Then, you can choose whether or not you want to *use* the identity. Of course, you can abandon the identity and deny who you are. Or, you can embody it and embrace the reality that you *are* an Empath, and you can begin using great strategies and tools to thrive in life, rather than to live in fear.

Still, before you embody the new label, you really want to make sure that you completely identify. Knowing for certain is essential as it helps us embody who we are and feel more complete in our identity. So, I want you to take a read through the following story. If you relate to it, then you should check over the "Empath Checklist" after the story. If the story doesn't fully relate to you, that's okay, still read the Empath Checklist and see if you can relate to that. Some Empaths have better protection abilities than others.

Do You Relate to This?
You are parked in front of the post office. It's a day like any other: ordinary, plain, and simple. You have nothing big planned, other than to get this package sitting next to you off to your friend. You look down

at it and place your hand on top of it. It's time to go in, but you're not ready. Inside, you feel silly. *"It's just the post office!"* you try to rationalize and reason with yourself. *"Look, everyone is walking in and out like it's no big deal. Why are you so afraid?"* you continue, trying to give yourself a pep talk so you can get up and get going.

You subconsciously count the people as they walk in and out. On the surface, you know this is a simple task. Inside, you are constantly analyzing. Each time a person walks in, you can see their energy and emotions. You have their story in your mind, even though you are not entirely certain as to how it got there. When they walk out, you breathe a sigh of relief in knowing that there is one less energy in the building. Still, you are analyzing. You pay attention to how they leave, what they seem to be feeling, and the rest of the story falls into place in your mind. *"That guy is clearly upset..."* you think to yourself, noticing someone walking in through the door again. Although he does not seem obviously and outwardly upset, you can sense that there is something in his energy keeping him down. Anxiety crawls in as you think about having to enter the building where he, and many others, are filled up with emotions and energies that are overwhelming. You try one last time to get out of your car, but it feels like you can't. *"Come on, this is just anxiety! You got this, let's go!"* you repeat, over and over. On some level, you know it's not anxiety that is holding you back. It's not *you* holding you back at all. It's *them*. All of them. All of their energies raging through, overwhelming the space and causing you to feel stressed out. You know the moment you go stand in line you are going to be analyzing and processing. Only, this time you will not be shielded by the safety of your car. This time, they will begin to notice you and look at you. When they do, you can't help but catch eye contact. And when that happens, well, then you can read the whole story. The energies that swirl inside of you become too much to bear, especially when so many people seem to be staring directly *into* you. You don't know how they do it. You don't know how you notice it. But you know that when you connect with these people, even when there is zero conversation shared, you connect on an insanely deep level. Every. Single. Time.

So instead, you sit in your car with your hand on the package, giving yourself a pep talk. When you are ready, you will hop out and get the package sent. Then, you will be back in your car. Physically, you may appear fine. Your breath may be normal and steady, your heart rate may be calm and even. But inside *somewhere*, you will feel like you are gasping for air and like your heart is racing a mile per minute. That is because your energy is bared to the world and you can feel it, but you do not yet know how to protect it. You are an Empath in need of the energetic tools required to protect yourself and face the world with the ability to possess and *use* your gift, rather than feeling relentlessly abused by it.

Empath Checklist

If you relate to the above scenario, then there is a good chance that you are an Empath. Many Empaths are diagnosed with anxiety and depressive disorders because of how they experience the world around them. Being an Empath does not mean that you do not actually possess these disorders. Rather, it means that you may now have a reason as to *why*.

In addition to anxiety and stress, there are many other things that you may face if you are an Empath. Check off every one that is a "yes" for you.

	You seem to just "know" things even when no one has told you.
	When you know things, it's far beyond intuition or gut reaction. It is a pure, undeniable knowingness. The more you acknowledge it, the stronger it becomes.
	You are overwhelmed by public places.
	You might have certain public places that have a specific energy to them that you love, so you spend more time in these places. They help you recharge.
	When there are too many people around, something unidentifiable inside of you feels "loud."
	When someone around you feels something, you feel it too.
	If someone describes a feeling (physical or emotional), you immediately begin feeling it in your own body or emotions.

	You seem to know people's stories without ever asking or being told.
	You can tell what other people are thinking about you.
	When you see violence or cruelty you feel physically, emotionally, and mentally unwell.
	You may have stopped watching many TV shows and paying attention to the news and media altogether to prevent these painful feelings.
	You can't stand being around bad/negative energy.
	You may now watch a lot of comedies and innocent romance movies and shows that have no violence or true pain in them because they help you feel good.
	If someone is lying, you know.
	If someone is not telling you something, you know.
	When someone is sick or hurt, you may begin to have the same symptoms, even if you come out completely healthy on medical tests.
	If people are pregnant, you may feel sympathy pains or false pregnancies.
	You may have chronic digestive disorders. (This is caused by emotional overwhelm.)
	You may have chronic back, neck and shoulder problems. (From "carrying the weight of the world.")
	It may feel like you are magnetically attracted to the underdog and are always in the right place at the right time to help them.
	You may feel like it is your duty to look out for the underdog, so you do not necessarily mind the previous "symptom."
	You may look out for the underdogs to the point of being overwhelmed and no longer looking after yourself. This can be from looking out for one far too much or looking out for far too many.
	If someone is pained, you will help them. This is true even if they are not willing to admit their pain and they are toxic. Because you know what they are unwilling to admit, you want to "save" them and sometimes (or often) find yourself in painful or abusive situations.

	It may feel like everyone wants to talk to you about their problems.
	When everyone talks to you about your problems, it may make you feel like you have many even if you do not.
	You may feel chronically tired. Sleep may not feel like it provides you with enough proper rest, so you feel like you are constantly too tired.
	You may have an addictive personality, finding yourself drawn to binging on drugs, alcohol, sex, food, or anything else that allows you to feel good, even if only temporarily.
	Metaphysical things may seem fascinating to you: especially healing and holistic therapies.
	When you learn about metaphysical theories and practices, you likely find yourself unphased. Empaths rarely get shocked, even when these things seem "out there."
	You may be extremely creative. It is likely that your creativity is an outlet for you, even if you don't use it as often as you feel you should.
	You feel magnetically drawn to the outdoors, nature, and animals. These are essential in your life.
	You may feel like so much bad happens around you and in your life that it is hard to believe and appreciate the good things in your life.
	It feels like you need to be alone regularly, or all the time, otherwise it feels like life is "too much" for you.
	You wonder why other people can have thriving social lives and you can't seem to.
	You may find yourself regularly feeling bored or distracted if you are not being stimulated. If things are not interesting, you seem to just "switch off" and find yourself drawing or daydreaming.
	It may feel impossible to do anything you do not enjoy. This can make living a modern, socially "normal" life feel virtually impossible for you.
	You likely find yourself only interested in hearing the truth, to the point that everything you do is rooted in finding it.

	Adventure likely feels great to you. Being able to have freedom is important to you, so you find yourself traveling and adventuring through life regularly.
	You identify as a "free spirit."
	You cannot stand cluttered or dirty spaces because they make you feel overwhelmed inside.
	You love daydreaming, and you can spend hours doing it. To you, it's a hobby.
	Routine is imprisoning to you: you cannot stand trying to do the same thing over and over, day in and day out.
	You may find yourself overweight even though you do not overeat and you seem to have no medical issues causing it. (This is a subconscious way of protecting yourself from the outside world.)
	You are an incredible listener. You seem to know exactly what people are saying, even if they are struggling to tell you clearly.
	You have an intolerance toward narcissism, though you may find yourself being stuck around narcissists constantly.
	You can tell how the collective is feeling. Each day of the week, month, and holiday all have their own collective "energy," and you can tell how everyone seems to be doing that day on a collective level.
	You do not own any antique items because the energy associated with them is overwhelming. You would prefer to own new, unused items because they feel energetically "clean."
	You can tell how the energy of food is. You may find yourself unwilling to eat meats because the energy does not feel good to you.
	You can also sense the energy of vegetables and other foods. You may find yourself secretly thanking your food for all it does and feeling energetically attached to it.
	To others, you may appear moody, shy, introverted, or unapproachable. These mood swings are generally caused by taking on too much energy from others.

You Are An Empath

If most of these sounded very familiar to you and you checked most of the boxes above then you can be pretty confident that you are an Empath. Being an Empath is both an exciting and somewhat scary thing. On one hand, you now know what you are, and you can take the proper measures to take care of yourself. The energy that once crippled you sent you through rollercoasters of emotions and caused you to feel overwhelmed and "abnormal" can now be managed and handled. You can even use it as your superpower, helping you master what you are here to do, feel fulfilled, and thrive in life.

However, early on when people realize they are Empaths, they tend to feel overwhelmed. Suddenly, all of your regular symptoms may feel heightened. This is because you are now more aware of them and you are paying attention to them more than you ever have before. As a result, you may find that the next few weeks until you begin to really embody and embrace your protective and self-care skills are extra vulnerable and challenging. For that reason, it is a good idea to make sure that you begin practicing these protection and self-care practices as soon as possible and that you really integrate them into your life. The more you practice and use them, the easier it will become to rely on them and have trust in them. Then, they will begin to support you in having a happier and healthier life that is less overwhelming and isolating.

Chapter 2: What is An Empath?

"Empaths are multi-sensory beings who see "beyond the veil" of people's personas and feel other's innermost emotions as their own."
-   *Unknown*

Empaths are a form of highly sensitive individuals that are known for being able to energetically experience the energies of other individuals. Rather than simply experiencing the emotion of empathy, Empaths can emotionally, mentally, and physically sense and feel another person's experience. This enables Empaths to be highly sensitive toward other people. This is both a blessing and a curse, depending on how it is used and cared for by the Empath themselves.

What is an Empath?
An Empath is said to be a person who has a paranormal ability to actually "step into" the state of another individual. Empaths are highly sensitive beings who can literally sense and feel the emotions and feelings of other individuals. If an individual is an Empath, they can sense deep emotions beyond what someone else is actively expressing. This means that even if an individual is highly gifted at hiding their emotions or masking them with other emotions, an Empath can sense, feel, and intricately understand the true emotions of that individual. Not only can the Empath sense and feel these emotions, but they can also understand them on a deep level.

Empaths have the capacity to experience complete empathy toward virtually anyone and everyone else. They can sense it towards family, friends, associates, kids, strangers, animals, plants, and even inanimate objects. Some people are known to be more empathetic toward certain things over others. This is often how we end up with things like "animal whisperers" or "plant whisperers." When this happens, that particular person is known to be more empathetic toward that which they can supposedly "whisper" to. What is really happening is not a whisper, but instead a deep inner knowing of what the other's needs are.

If a person is an Empath, they are not restricted by time and space. In fact, they are not really restricted at all. An Empath can sense the emotions and mental state of people who are incredibly far away. Some can even sense the emotions and mental state of individuals who have long since passed. For example, if they were to visit a museum and see the belongings of someone who existed many years ago but whom has since passed away, some Empaths can step directly into the feelings and energies of that person. This enables Empaths to be deeply understanding and to have a highly unique perspective of the world around them.

Empaths are said to be "poets in motion." They see the world in a wonderfully creative and artistic way. They are generally highly artistic, creating art in every way imaginable. Some may master a particular art form, whereas others may prefer to dabble in a little bit of everything. Empaths see the world in a way that most others don't. To them, each day is a new chapter and the book needs to be written in the most poetic way possible.

An Empath can be virtually anyone. They are not known to be isolated to any particular gender, race, culture, or religion. Empaths exist anywhere and everywhere.

Scientific Explanation

From a scientific standpoint, Empaths are thought to have hyper-responsive mirror neurons. Mirror neurons are a group of specialized brain cells that are responsible for helping individuals feel compassion. These cells enable the individual to actually mirror the emotions of other individuals, allowing them to share directly in the other person's experience. Through these mirror neurons, Empaths can feel when other people are feeling things as well. For example, if your spouse is hurt, you may hurt as well. If your dog is elated, you may begin to feel elated as well. If a plant is thirsty, you may begin to feel thirsty as well.

This mirror neuron system allows individuals to experience high levels of empathy toward others, and it is believed that they are highly active in individuals who are considered highly sensitive Empaths.

Electromagnetic fields are generated by both the heart and the brain in individuals. It is believed that these fields are capable of transmitting information about an individual's thoughts and emotions to those around them. Empaths are believed to be highly sensitive to these electromagnetic fields and are capable of picking up on them and recognizing exactly what information is stored within these fields.

Another reason why Empaths are believed to be so sensitive toward other people is through emotional contagion. Emotional contagion was found in research that showed that people generally pick up on the emotions of those around them and then many will experience and express those emotions themselves. This is what causes an entire ward of babies to begin crying after just one baby cries for any particular reason. So, if one baby is upset because they are hungry and begins crying, the rest of the room will likely begin crying simply because they heard someone else crying. Though, later in life, many people learn to block out these feelings or stay focused on their own. Empaths however, can actually feel these emotions and will regularly experience and express them themselves as well, especially if they are unaware that they are being picked up from their environment and not personally created.

Shamanic Explanation
Shamans believe that Empaths are highly gifted healers. Because they have the capacity to sense and feel the emotions, thoughts, and physical experiences of those around them, Empaths are extremely talented at being able to create a deep connection toward others. This allows them to have an accurate understanding of what another person is going through, thus supporting them in creating and facilitating healing that will actually work for the other individual.

Many Shamans believe that Empaths are specifically meant to be healers. They believe that this is not just a gift they have, but a duty they have here on Earth. Shamans believe that being an Empath means your innate calling is as a healer and that you should pursue this life path. Through being an Empath, it is believed that you have the capacity to discover mental and physical illnesses in individuals in a unique and accurate manner, allowing you to facilitate healing that will truly provide healing to the other individual. When trained and refined, the skill of the Empath is extremely precise. They can also move into the energetic and emotional state of the other person without personally taking on the individual energies, allowing them to "step in" and "step out" of the other person's experience with the sole purpose of gathering information from them.

To follow the shamanistic lifepath of an Empathic healer, it is essential that an individual be properly trained. Operating as an energetic healer when you are an Empath can result in you being left wide open to energies that can drain and overwhelm you. It can also result in poor boundaries that leave you susceptible to being energetically attacked by energy vampires, narcissists, and others whom may lack empathy and are known to exploit those who have a plethora of it, such as Empaths.

Life and Spiritual Purpose of Empaths
Many believe that one of the biggest reasons Empaths are here on Earth is to promote and facilitate healing to the general collective. For years, Earth has been overrun by people who lack empathy and who are unable to feel genuine emotions for other people. These individuals are believed to be responsible for corrupting governments, creating a toxic corporate industry, and otherwise leading the human race in a very monotonous, emotionally-void manner that starves humans of their basic needs. It is believed that Empaths are here to protect us and save us from that.

Empaths often choose to pursue paths that align with some degree of healing. They will either focus their efforts on healing one individual at a time, such as with alternative energy healing practices or counseling, or they will focus their efforts on healing large organizations at a time, such as through massive charities or activism. These paths nourish the Empaths need to see the world doing better and to leave it a better place than it was when they arrived.

Although the exact life and spiritual paths of each Empath will vary slightly, the majority are here to heal and reawaken consciousness. They are actively working toward shifting us all toward a better society that supports each individual, promotes and honors emotional wellbeing, and allows us to thrive throughout our lifetimes.

As an Empath, seeing other people suffer and feeling incapable of doing anything about it is treacherous. It can lead to deep suffering for the Empath themselves, resulting in feelings of inner torture and depression. It is through this need to serve that many Empaths may find themselves getting caught up with narcissists, which you will learn more about during your self-assessment in Chapter 4.

The Gift of Being an Empath

If you have done any previous research on being an Empath, you may be fearful that you have been cursed rather than gifted. Many Empaths are presently experiencing a lot of darkness because they are not being properly trained in how to use their gifts. As a result, they are taking on a lot of dark and painful energies from the world around them. In shamanistic terms, they are stepping into other people's experiences, but are not trained in how to step back out. This can be highly overwhelming and painful.

However, the reality is that being an Empath is actually a gift. Once you begin to learn how to master your empathic abilities, you will discover that you have many talents that Earth deeply needs right now. This means you are highly valuable to us here on Earth! You are capable of supporting the collective consciousness in healing, allowing us to rise to a new state of society where we are all nourished, honored, and supported for our experiences here on Earth. Slowly, as a result of all of the Empaths here working toward our betterment, we will begin to witness positive shifts in major areas of our society. The government, corporate, and many other bodies of society who have been known to have a reputation of being greedy, corrupted, and selfish will all begin to shift toward a healthier and more socially conscious style.

Being an Empath means you are not like the rest of the people who are continually abusing and destroying Earth and everyone and everything

25

that lies in their path. It means that you are here to heal and save us from these experiences. It may feel like a massive burden, but understand that it is actually a gift to be proud of. And, since more and more Empaths are incarnating on Earth at this time, you now have access to a great support system that can help you in bringing your missions into completion in reality. You will no longer have to hope and pray for better outcomes because you and the rest of the Empaths that you connect with will all work together to bring a brighter future to Earth and all who inhabit it.

Chapter 3: Empath Archetypes

"I believe Empathy is the most essential quality of civilization."
- *Roger Ebert*

The word "Empath" itself refers to individuals who are highly sensitive toward others. However, there are actually different types of Empaths who exist. These are known as "Empath archetypes." In this chapter, we are going to explore the different archetypes. See if you can identify with any of these to begin exploring what archetype of Empath you may be.

Emotional Empath

One of the most common archetypes of Empaths is the emotional Empath archetype. Emotional Empaths are known to easily pick up on the emotions of those around them, allowing them to feel the effects of the emotions as if they were yours. This can result in you deeply experiencing the emotional body of others, potentially even expressing and feeling these emotions as if they truly were your own emotions.

As an emotional Empath, your most common symptoms will be that you seemingly randomly pick up emotions that make no sense. For example, say you are shopping at the mall, and there is someone in the same store as you that is feeling intense sadness. You may pick up on this and feel an overwhelming need to cry despite not having a strong understanding of or reason for why this is happening.

Another thing emotional Empaths tend to feel symptoms from is their living arrangements. As an emotional Empath, you may find yourself feeling victimized by the people you live with. Family members or housemates who have overwhelming energies or emotions may create distress for you in your own home. For many Empaths, this can make being at home feel unsafe and uncomfortable. For example, if you have a housemate who has a tendency to be angry and unhappy with their life, you may find yourself regularly picking up on their anger. For you this can resonate as anger within yourself, feeling as though you are now angry as well even though you may not entirely understand why. Furthermore, you may find yourself feeling scared because the amount of anger you feel and the power behind it may feel overwhelming. Therefore, whenever that particular housemate comes home, you may find yourself feeling stressed out, scared, and unwilling to participate in household activities. Simple things such as going into the bathroom to shower or going into the kitchen to get water may feel overwhelming. For some, it may even feel like you are constantly trying to hide from that person to avoid feeling their energy. Even though you can feel it from afar anyway, you want to minimize how much you feel by creating some level of distance between you.

For any human, this type of living condition can be overwhelming and stressful. It can create a sense of feeling like you do not belong anywhere and feeling like there is nowhere safe for you to be. Home is a place where you should feel comfortable to hang your hat and find peace and quiet. It should feel like a sanctuary where you can relax and recharge, not a place where you have to be on your toes constantly prepared to deal with any emotional outbreak that may come your way.

When it comes to being an emotional Empath, it is important that you take the time to learn how you can differentiate between your own emotions and the emotions of other people. If you are not actively capable of doing this, you may begin to feel as though your Empathic abilities are burdensome because you are exhausted from being on an emotional roller coaster that almost certainly does not belong to you. Seeking support and enforcing tools that can assist you in recognizing your own emotions versus the emotions of others can be extremely valuable in supporting your ability to master your Empathic abilities.

Physical or Medical Empath

Empaths that are capable of picking up on the physical sensations and symptoms of others and feeling them within their own bodies are known to be physical Empaths. These Empaths may follow the path of becoming a medical Empath because they have an easier time recognizing and diagnosing ailments in individuals due to their ability to feel what their patient is feeling.

28

As a physical Empath, you will recognize symptoms such as being able to feel sensations of an ailment that someone is describing to you. For example, if your friend complains that they have a headache, you may immediately begin to feel a headache coming on. This is because you are picking up on the sensations that your friend is experiencing. This does not have to be verbalized, however, for your gift to activate. For example, if someone is in your vicinity who has cancer, you may be able to tell and know exactly who it is without ever having been informed of this ailment, simply because you can feel and sense it.

When you are a physical Empath, it is important that you learn to ground and connect to your own sensations to refrain from feeling and holding onto every single ailment that you hear about or connect to. If you are not careful, you may feel as though you are in a chronic state of pain. Many physical Empaths will be diagnosed with chronic pain conditions such as fibromyalgia for this very reason.

Geomantic Empath
If you are a geomantic Empath, this means that you can attune to the energies and emotions in an environment or place. So, certain places may make you overwhelmingly happy even though you may have been feeling completely neutral coming into the place. Alternatively, some may give you an overwhelming feeling of sadness, anger, frustration, uncertainty, fear, or otherwise. These are all symptoms of being tapped into your environment and drawing on emotions and energies from it.

Empaths who are attuned to geomantic energies regularly need to spend time in nature to relieve themselves from the energies they are experiencing. Being in nature can support them in feeling calm and comfortable, allowing them to rest and recharge so that they can go back into the world and feel safe and secure.

Plant Empath
Plant Empaths are exactly what they sound like: individuals who are highly attuned to plant energy. Individuals who are known to be plant Empaths seem to naturally have a green thumb, being able to easily

care for any plant effortlessly with minimal support or prior information. Individuals who are plant Empaths can sense what a plant needs or wants, allowing them to find the perfect environment for that plant to grow in, as well as in knowing when to feed and water the plants.

If you are a plant Empath, you may feel like you receive guidance directly from trees and plants. This is typically sensed by hearing or knowing what they are trying to transmit to you within your mind. As a plant Empath, you may find that you pick up information directly pertaining to the plant's needs, as well as wisdom about life in general. Keeping a lot of contact with plants and trees and spending time in forested nature is a great way to keep your Empathic senses nourished and grounded.

Animal Empath

While virtually every Empath has a strong connection with animals, animal Empaths have an incredibly powerful one. Individuals who are animal Empaths will generally devote their entire lives to animals in one way or another. They may do this by becoming an animal whisperer or behavioral trainer, taking care of animals through volunteering at organizations, or even becoming veterinarians.

Animal Empaths typically spend as much time with animals as possible as this supports them in feeling connected to their purpose in life. They may find the study of the biology or psychology of animals to be fascinating, possibly even pursuing it to support their mission of supporting animals in every way possible. Because of their gifts, animal Empaths are especially capable of talking to animals in a paranormal way, as well as discovering what ailment they may be facing so that they can promote healing within the animal.

Claircognizant or Intuitive Empath

Intuitive Empaths are known to be claircognizant. This means that they intuitively "know" when something is going on. They can easily detect when people are lying to them, they are able to sense the true emotions and intentions of others, and they can draw information from virtually any person, place, or thing. These individuals are talented at "just knowing" when something is up. Many might claim that they have a strong gut sense or sixth sense that supports them in reading their environment to get accurate feedback from it. Most empaths have these abilities to an extent but not to the level of an Intuitive Empath.

If you are an intuitive Empath, you will also need to make sure that you learn how to step back out of experiences after you have stepped in. You may find yourself stepping into other people's experiences accidentally or naturally, particularly if you are not trained. Knowing how to step back out will allow you to "turn off" the inner voice from time to time so that you can ground and enjoy your reality in addition to being able to use your Empathic gifts as needed.

The Wounded Healer

The wounded healer is a secondary archetype. This means that you can be any other one of the archetypes (or even multiple) and then have this archetype as well. Unlike the others, however, this archetype can be healed. In fact, if you recognize that you have it, it should be healed.

Wounded healers are individuals whom are believed to have suffered a great deal of misery and trauma for their Empathic gifts in past lives. They may have also suffered within this life time too. As a result, they have grown to see their gift as a curse and may feel drawn to attempt to sabotage it or hide it to refrain from being further hurt. This actually hurts the Empath even more, resulting in them not feeling empowered to pursue their life and spiritual missions. Some common symptoms of a wounded healer include: hiding their gift, viewing their gift as a curse, undervaluing themselves when sharing their gift, sharing their gift with the wrong people, or otherwise allowing their gift to essentially curse them.

Healing the wounded healer archetype comes from spending time understanding what caused this secondary archetype to arise in the first place. Then, once you have, you can begin to heal accordingly. If this is from vows you have taken in past lives, you can work together with a past life regression healer who can support you in breaking these vows and empowering your current life. If these are from undervaluing yourself due to being disempowered during your current life, you may want to work together with another healer who does not presently suffer from the wounded healer archetype that can support you in feeling more empowered within your gifts again.

The wounded healer is extremely common and there is no shame in realizing that you may suffer from this secondary archetype. If you do, be sure to seek support in releasing it and know that you are not always going to feel this poorly or wounded around your gifts. You *can* feel empowered once more. There will also be more information on overcoming this later in the book.

Chapter 4: Self-Assessment: Are You An Empath?

"Your sensitivity is one of your greatest superpowers. "
- *Unknown*

Now that you have begun to understand more about what an Empath is and the various types of Empaths, it is time to determine whether or not you are one. If you are reading this book and feeling connected to it already, there is a good chance that the answer is "YES!" However, let's take a deeper exploration to see how Empath-like you truly are. The following list is filled with phenomena that Empaths regularly experience. If you feel that you connect to many, most, or all of these phenomena, then there is a good chance that your Empathic gift is extremely strong. In other words, you are extremely gifted!

You Are A Great Listener

Empaths are known to be incredible listeners. In fact, many tend to be the "counselor" in their friend group. You may notice that your friends, family, loved ones, and maybe even complete strangers come to you with their problems and want to talk. At times, it may even feel like you are an emotional dumping ground for people's thoughts and emotions.

As an Empath, you have a strong ability to listen to others and truly feel what they are sharing with you. They especially like talking to you because people feel like you hear what they *aren't* saying and know the problem better than they do, which can be a great relief for many. Modern society is not overly accepting of many thoughts, feelings, or emotions. As a result, many people are uncomfortable or seemingly incapable of sharing these things. Because you seem to "just know," people may be drawn to you because it feels like a breath of fresh air being understood in ways that no one has likely ever understood them before.

You May Struggle to Connect to Standard Religion

Many Empaths find it extremely challenging to connect to the teachings of the majority of modern religions. Although most Empaths will see and appreciate the underlying messages of connection and unconditional love, they tend to pick up on the reality that most religious organizations do not actually live or operate in alignment with these teachings. This can lead to a deep inner sense of struggle for any Empaths who have been raised in or around a religious community. They *want* to see the good in it all and connect with their loved ones, but many see right through the teachings and find themselves feeling frustrated with the deception that seems to go on with many religious groups. Furthermore, Empaths highly value freedom and free will, both of which are rarely honored in religious teachings. For this reason, most Empaths will find themselves being heavily drawn away from religious teachings, perhaps even growing a deep sense of resentment toward them and all that they stand for.

You Are Drawn to Spirituality

Despite not being attracted to religious teachings, many Empaths will be attracted to spirituality. Spirituality tends to be more accepting of and understanding toward Empaths, allowing them to feel understood and recognized by others. This also allows them to facilitate deep connections toward the teachings and the others who follow similar paths. This type of connection can be heavily empowering for Empaths, allowing them to feel supported in their journey as they also support others. Since the spiritual path is filled with Empaths, many Empaths trust that the individuals in these journeys will think similarly to them and therefore will be more accepting, understanding, empathetic, compassionate, and caring towards them. This allows them to feel reciprocated, making it far more inviting than many standard religious teachings.

In addition to supporting them in feeling understood, many spirituality-based teachings actually elaborate on the meaning of being an Empath and support Empaths in understanding themselves and refining their talents. This means that through these teachings the Empath can further their own sense of self-understanding and work more passionately alongside their life and spiritual purposes with clear direction, guidance, and support.

You Struggle to Keep Healthy Boundaries

One symptom many Empaths face is struggling to keep healthy boundaries. Because an Empath can sense exactly what another person is feeling or experiencing, they may find themselves regularly making excuses for the other person. Things such as "oh, they didn't mean to" or "they only did this because deep down they are hurting" regularly come to mind. Although having these deep understandings of others can be valuable, they can also result in the Empath being taken advantage of and used by others with less empathy, or none at all.

The difficulty of maintaining healthy boundaries, or any boundaries at all, for Empaths, can be a major point of trauma. Because the Empath strives to see the good in others, they may let people repeatedly take advantage of them or abuse them because they struggle to connect to the reality that you cannot help someone who does not want to help themselves. You may feel like you have to be the "savior," even though the chances of this panning out are extremely slim.

You May Struggle with Addictions

Empaths are known to struggle with addictions. Many use addictions as a coping method to attempt to "shut off" their empathy or numb them toward the world around them. While this may seem to work, the reality is that nothing can actually shut off their gift. Instead, what often ends up happening is that they begin to dissociate from their feelings and ignore the reality of their empathic abilities. Over time, this leads to a deep sense of depression because they take on an excessive amount of energy and emotion, create even more within themselves, and never effectively deal with or release any of these energies or emotions.

Addictions within Empaths are not restricted to substance abuse. They may also be drawn to overeating, oversleeping or never sleeping to avoid nightmares and restlessness, video games, or otherwise obsessively attempting to draw their attention away from reality to avoid the pain that they are experiencing and suffering with.

You Are Likely Highly Creative

Individuals who are empathic are almost always highly creative. They perceive the world in an entirely different way and tend to see art where others see virtually nothing. For example, an Empath may look at a blank page and see an entire image come to life, thus drawing them into wanting to create that image and bring it into reality. Empaths have visual gifts unlike any other, allowing them to quite literally think things into existence. An individual who is not empathic would likely see just a page that is blank. Empaths are known to become artists on varying levels. They may create art through words, objects, perception, photography, or virtually anything else. The entire world is a canvas to Empaths, and they just want to create. Creating allows them to express themselves in ways that words and emotions do not always allow for. Additionally, it gives them the opportunity to feel incredible self-worth, empowered and inspired by the world around them.

You Can "Feel" Others

People who are empathic can "feel" others. As you may have picked up on in previous chapters, this is actually one of the primary things that identify an Empath. If you can feel others either emotionally, mentally, or physically, or any combination of these three, there is a good chance that you are an Empath. These symptoms allow you to step into the reality of others and experience what they are experiencing in a way that the average person cannot.

When it comes to Empathy, average people experiencing Empathy can relate what someone else is experiencing to something that they have experienced themselves in the past. However, for an Empath, it is much deeper than that. You do not relate people to your own experiences. Instead, you directly feel theirs. This is what allows Empaths to feel things that they have never personally experienced before. For example, if someone were to tell you that they had a concussion, you may feel the exact symptoms they are experiencing even if you have never had a concussion before.

You May Have Suffered from Narcissistic Abuse

Narcissists are drawn to Empaths because they have the one thing that the narcissist completely lacks: empathy. Empaths, as you know, have a heightened level of empathy that is above average. This makes them more desirable than the average person because they have enough to substitute for the lack of empathy that the narcissist has. Furthermore, Empaths are more likely to forgive and desire to see the good in other people. This means that it is easy for a narcissist to draw Empaths into their abuse cycles and quickly turn their empathic gift into a burden that they long to destroy so that they can step away.

If you have ever suffered from narcissistic abuse, or if you are currently suffering from narcissistic abuse, it may be because you are an Empath. If you feel that you are and would actively like support in helping you safely escape and heal from this abuse, or retrospectively understand what was happening during that time in your life, you may be interested in reading my other book: *"Emotional and Narcissistic Abuse: The Complete Survival Guide to Understanding Narcissism, Escaping the Narcissist in a Toxic Relationship Forever, and Your Road to Recovery."*

You May Feel Extremely Close to Plants and Animals

Empaths, especially plant Empaths and animal Empaths, have a tendency to feel extremely close to plants and animals. Even if you are not a plant or animal Empath, you may still find yourself feeling extremely drawn to them. This is because they tend to have a much purer energy, filled with unconditional love. For many Empaths, plants and animals are a breath of fresh air from the corrupted society that many of us live in.

If you find that you are heavily drawn to plants and animals, and especially if you feel like you can communicate with them in a paranormal way, this may be an indication that you are experiencing your empathic gifts. The unconditional love you feel between each other is
simply amazing and blissful. You may even feel that your plants and pets are the only things that can make you feel better when things are not going well. If you feel that you receive wisdom and advice from plants and animals, this is your claircognizant gift arising from your empathic abilities.

You Might Have Experienced Mental or Physical Symptoms

Empaths often experience mental and physical symptoms relating to their gift, in addition to the more commonly talked about emotional symptoms. These are not always directly borrowed from someone else, but may actually be the symptom of feeling so many other people's energies so deeply. Many Empaths may actually experience psychotic attacks or episodes because they feel overwhelmed by the amount of energy around them that they are constantly picking up on. Often, Empaths feel like they are a "sponge" to the world around them, which can result in them picking up and holding on to a lot of different sensations.

Some of the common mental or physical symptoms that you are likely to face are those that are related to experiencing chronic high stress. The body can only carry so many different energies and emotions before it becomes too much for it. Then, it begins to maximize its output of cortisol, the stress hormone, causing for you to begin experiencing emotional, mental, and physical symptoms related to personal stress. This could be anything from physical pain to anxiety and depression, and even chronic thoughts based on suicide or self-harm. It is important to understand that these symptoms are often in relation to your empathic gift. They are generally heightened by both you experiencing other people's stress, as well as the stress from feeling these feelings without properly managing them within yourself. In other words, you are not stepping out so the stress is getting blocked within you.

You May Experience Psychic Attacks
Psychic attacks are a common experience for individuals who are Empathic. Psychic attacks are an attack on Empaths with negative energy. This energy is sent either consciously or unconsciously by another individual or entity with the intention of creating or inflicting harm upon said person. These attacks can be felt by anyone in your life, including family and friends, an acquaintance, or in some cases entities that we cannot see. This harm can be intended to create turmoil in the emotional, spiritual, physical, or mental state of the individual receiving the attack.

If you have ever had a psychic attack, you would recognize it through a multitude of symptoms that you might face. One of these symptoms includes feeling exhausted and then having a deep sleep where you may or may not remember having a nightmare. You may have fears in your dreams of being attacked by someone, typically with quite a large amount of violence. You may also feel extreme and unrealistic fears that feel debilitating. There may be no rational explanation as to why you have this fear or why it is so strong for you, all you know is that you suddenly have it. You may also begin feeling much better following a bath or shower as they support you in protecting your energy and freeing yourself from psychic attack. It may feel like you are not in control over yourself or your thoughts which may lead to increased fear.

Psychic attacks feel a lot like psychotic attacks, causing you to feel like you are no longer lucid and in full control of your own body. Many reports they feel like they are standing next to themselves watching themselves go through the motions. While this may be medically rooted, if you are an Empath there is also a large chance that you are experiencing a psychic attack. These attacks are essentially caused by someone else's energy invading into your personal energy space, causing you to begin feeling unwell and even damaged by their energy.

If you are having or have been exposed to a psychic attack, you need to read *Chapter 9: Empathic Protection* and begin protecting yourself from other people's energies. I would also highly recommend seeing a Shaman. A Shaman will be able to understand what is going on from an energetic point of view and be able to deal with the root cause.

You Are Sensitive to Food

Empaths are known to feel their food in a way that no one else can. Many will become vegetarian or vegan because they feel too much negative energy in meats and animal byproducts. However, this is not always the case. Other people find that they can eat meat just fine as long as it has been ethically sourced. Some also like to bless their meat before eating. How you choose your diet will be highly personal, but you may find that it is chosen based on the feeling and energy of the food more so than anything else.

When you are empathic, you may find that you can literally feel what you need. For example, say your energies are feeling off, you may feel that you need the energy that is within carrots, sweet potatoes, or other foods. This comes from your energetic capacity to read your own energy, read the energy of your food, and discover what it is that you need exactly. You may also feel energetically averted to things that may be causing chaos or destruction within your body. For example, you may be naturally averted to sugars and sweets, especially when you are feeling under the weather because your body knows what energy it does and does not need at any given time.

Other Empaths report feeling emotions from their food. For example, they may feel joy and a surge of love and passion when they look at a plate full of foods that give them positive energy. However, they may feel dreadful and even nauseous when they look at a plate of food that seems to radiate negative energy. Being able to feel the energy in their food means Empaths can intuitively eat in a way that nourishes their body well.

You Can Feel Collective Energy

Collective energy is something that typically only Empaths can feel. Empaths will recognize collective energy based on any number of things. For example, if a large-scale tragedy happens such as natural disasters, Empaths can sense and feel the energy of the collective during that time. There may be a large, unavoidable "void" or sense of loss and longing that arises in the Empath. Alternatively, if it is Friday, they may feel a sense of joy and excitement because the collective collectively look forward to the weekend and so the energy of that day is higher. This will be true for the Empath even if Friday is not the last day of work before the weekend for them. For example, stay at home parents or parents who work through the weekend will still feel this excitement if they are Empathic.

Many things can influence collective energy, and Empaths can tune in and sense and feel those things. Their ability to recognize how the general population will be on an energetic level gives them the capacity to read and understand their environment on any given day. This is how the Empath is able to understand the needs of those around them and how they can expect to look forward to the day.

Unfortunately, this can also lead to a deep sense of emotional turmoil for the Empath. For example, if an Empath is tuned into unwanted or uncomfortable energies, they may begin to feel excessively moody even if they are not being directly impacted by anything that is impacting the collective consciousness.

This is actually why many Empaths are finding themselves overwhelmed, stressed, and even traumatized in the modern world. With so much war, fighting, tragedy, and hate crimes swirling around everywhere, many Empaths feel overwhelmed and overburdened by their gifts. You can learn more about this in *Chapter 11: Ascending Earth Consciousness*.

You May Sense Bad Things Before They Happen

Because an Empath can sense and read the energy of individuals and collective, many find that they can actually detect when something bad is about to happen. They may have an unknowing sense of something being wrong, thus creating a sense of discomfort and distress within the Empath. When this happens, the Empath may begin to feel physically, mentally, and emotionally unwell. Often, restlessness will arise as they wait for the "other shoe to drop."

In some cases, the Empath may be able to intuitively sense where the bad news or tragedy is coming from. However, in most cases, the Empath will simply know that something bad is going to happen. This can be extremely troubling as they are unsure as to what to expect or what to look for. Instead, they simply know that something bad will happen. This can be troubling for anyone, but especially for an Empath who can literally feel the trouble rising.

For the majority of times, the Empath's sense that something bad is going to happen is confirmed. It may be by something fairly small, such as their bank card not working when they are at the gas station, or for something large such as a fatality or a traumatic event. Either way, it is very seldom that an Empath will genuinely feel that something is going to happen and then find themselves wrong in their feeling.

Truth Seekers

Empaths strive to know the truth. They want to have a deep sense of inner knowingness. As a result of being able to know things so deeply and purely, they crave to know *everything* on this level, especially things that they are interested in. When they don't, it can be troubling for the Empath. They may find themselves stressed out, searching for the truth and trying to find that sense of understanding. This can manifest in many ways, including anything from soul-searching to a lifelong dedication to education and studying. By consuming as much knowledge as they possibly can, Empaths give themselves the opportunity to discover information and create a sense of understanding within themselves that satisfies their hunger.

When an Empath does not know the complete truth about something they must know and they do not feel that deep sense of understanding, they will go to extreme lengths to find out. Nothing will be able to get in their way and they will keep 'hunting' until they find the information they have been searching for. Where the average person would usually give up after no success, the Empath persists.

Empaths can feel things incredibly deeply. When they don't, they will often feel empty. Truth enables the Empath to feel full. When they feel full, they are able to feel satisfied and go about life in a way that allows them to genuinely thrive. For that reason, virtually every Empath will be on a lifelong path of knowing and finding the truth. These truths may not always be verified by scientific or factual evidence, though. They may instead be verified by that deep knowingness that the Empath has, allowing them to know within themselves that they are right and that they have landed on the truth. *Their* truth.

If You Don't Love It, You Don't Do It

For an Empath, doing anything they do not love or at least agree with can be extremely challenging. If you find yourself struggling to stay committed to the things you don't love, especially when you also don't agree with them, there is a good chance that this is your empathic gift shining through. Empaths need to feel emotionally invested in all that they do. They want to love what they set out to do. For that reason, many will feel unwell or unhappy in their lives until they find what they love and pursue it.

If you find that you are literally unable to do the things you don't love doing, this is also likely caused by being an Empath. For you, it may feel untrue or unaligned to do the things that you do not love doing. The Empath needs to be feel congruent. Inside, you rationalize this by realizing that there is only one guaranteed life that you have here on Earth and you do not want to waste it being miserable and taking on the energy of avoidance, resentment, and unhappiness.

You are not alone in feeling like you cannot do these things. A way to overcome this is to find a way to love it or make it fun or to find a way to outsource the task. The best option though is to choose a different life path that allows you to have more joy and excitement, and less frustration and depression in your life.

You Often Feel Bored or Distracted

This ties in with the previous trait. Empaths have a deep need to be stimulated. Feeling deeply is almost addicting, allowing them to have a rush of energy and emotion in a way that can only be understood by other Empaths. If you find yourself regularly feeling unfulfilled and thus becoming bored or distracted easily, it may be because you are empathic. In fact, many Empaths are even diagnosed with ADD, ADHD, and other attention disorders. This is caused by their need to *feel*.

If you are often bored or distracted, you need to find things to do that cause you to feel deeply. Many Empaths find great success in reading, watching movies, creating, playing sports, and engaging in relationships that offer great emotional depth. Having access to that capacity to feel, at least most of the time, can help you stay focused when you need to. Whenever you can, make sure that even ordinary everyday tasks have been optimized for feeling. For example, if you need to vacuum, choose a vacuum that brings you great joy or finds a way to make it a game that allows you to feel fulfilled and satisfied. Alternatively, multitask with something that fills you up, such as listening to music or audiobooks. Having at least one aspect of mundane tasks infused with things that help you feel will make it easier for you to stay committed.

You Want to Heal Others

Empaths have a magnetic feeling toward their need to heal others. Many believe that Empaths came here as healers which is why they have this feeling. Because Empaths can feel how deeply humanity and society have been traumatized and "broken," they feel a deep longing and urge to heal this damage. This, according to many, is the true purpose of the Empath. To sense where society is broken and repair the damage so that we can be restored to a society of love and joy.

If you find yourself being called to heal others, this may be as a result of your Empathic calling. Pursuing skills that will support you in healing others, such as alternative medicine, energy healing, counselling, or otherwise, will help you put this healing call to work. Then, you can begin feeling fulfilled by doing work that genuinely calls to your heart and makes you feel as though you are doing what you came here to do. For an Empath, that feeling is both addicting and necessary. That deep sense of fulfilling reminds Empaths why they are here and that their gifts are truly gifts and not burdens.

Chapter 5: Growing Up Empathic

"It's not our job to toughen our children up to face a cruel and heartless world. It's our job to raise children who will make this world a little less cruel and heartless."
-   **L.R. Knost**

If you are an Empath, you have been one since birth. For that reason, growing up as an Empath could have been challenging for you. Many Empaths are not adequately supported throughout their childhood, resulting in them feeling disempowered and believing that something is wrong with them. Some will even push to their doctors to test them to ensure that they are not suffering from some form of emotional or personality disorder.

Growing Up as An Empath

Many who grow up as an Empath feel that there is something different about them that other people do not tend to experience. They often grow up feeling overly sensitive and like their emotional symptoms are not well-understood by others in society. Because society is not well-designed for Empaths, it can result in them feeling as though there are not enough resources available for Empathic children to understand themselves and their intense feelings. This generally leads to two things: bullying, and rejecting themselves.

Being unable to know how to emotionally convey yourself in a way that is considered "normal" to society can result in feeling like you are fundamentally wrong. Empathic children often find themselves struggling with low self-esteem issues, low confidence, and difficulty in socializing with others. This is especially present in socializing with the opposite sex. They may find themselves attempting to have a normal childhood but regularly becoming outcast or shunned for their extra sensitives. This can result in them feeling as though they are incapable of fitting in because they do not communicate and share in the same way that the other children do. That is where the bullying and traumatic events can begin to arise for children.

When Empaths are not taught how to handle their energies and symptoms, they can appear to be oversensitive and weak to others. Children in their schools who are not empathic themselves may pick up on these sensitivities and begin to exploit them. This can result in bullying, sometimes in severe cases. As a child, you may have found yourself a victim of bullying that has had lasting, severe consequences for your mental health. Because there are very few resources available to the empathic child, there is not a lot available for them to learn how to manage their emotions and energies and protect themselves against bullying and the many additional energetic challenges that it presents. If you had this experience in your childhood, you might have felt as though you had a lot of care for the others in your school but that no one reciprocated this care. This can lead to feeling like something is fundamentally wrong with you, and like you are an anomaly that will never be loved or appreciated by others. It also means that you will need to go on and rewire these parts of your brain in adulthood to eliminate the traumatic impact the bullying had on you and give yourself the chance to (finally) be free from the bullying. Many empathic children go on to devalue themselves and develop the wounded healer archetype through childhood traumas such as this.

The other side of not having adequate resources to support and educate empathic children is that there are very few ways for these children to develop a complete understanding of themselves. As a result, many will reject the empathic self and attempt to assimilate into "normal" childhood activities. They may begin acting the part of the bully or otherwise behaving in a way that deeply rejects their overly caring side so that they can fit in. This leads to many challenges for the child, including deep feelings of self-rejection and all of the challenges that this type of experience brings along with it.

Feeling unaccounted for, unrecognized, and abnormal in your childhood as an Empath is completely normal. Although it is not a nice or desirable experience, it does happen for the vast majority of empathic children. This is not because there is anything fundamentally wrong with them, but rather because they are simply not understood enough and therefore they are not given the depth of support required to help them feel understood and "normal" as they are.

If you grew up with a classic empathic childhood, you might find that you are now struggling with symptoms of depression, anxiety, and other trauma-related symptoms. These symptoms are completely natural results when you are raised in this way. The reality is, in many cases, there was no way of preventing these things from happening because society can be rough on a child that is extra sensitive. Without access to the right information and knowledge, there was likely no way for you or others in your life to provide you with the support that you needed to successfully grow up empathic without coming out with some degree of emotional repercussions.

The goal now is to learn how to unwire these repercussions from your mind so that you can rewire it in a way that honors and nurtures your sensitivity, rather than making it feel like a. In other words, the tools that you failed to receive in childhood can now be learned and implemented in adulthood to support you in leading a better life where you can truly begin to thrive.

If You Had a Narcissistic Parent

Another side of the coin that is extremely common in Empath children's childhoods is being raised by a narcissistic parent. An overwhelming number of Empaths claim that they were raised in a narcissistic household that lead to a great deal of damage in their lives. Because Empaths are naturally susceptible to the psychological abuse inflicted by narcissists, being raised in a narcissistic household can further damage the child. Since the abuse starts right from a young age, these Empaths are conditioned to use their gift only for the benefit of serving narcissists. They are never granted the ability to see how this gift is powerful and what they can do with it. Instead, they are conditioned to accept the abuse from a young age and often will go on to find themselves being abused by more narcissists later in life. I discuss this topic far more in-depth regarding romantic relationships in my book *"Emotional and Narcissistic Abuse: The Complete Survival Guide to Understanding Narcissism, Escaping the Narcissist in a Toxic Relationship Forever, and Your Road to Recovery,"* detailing how the victims of these relationships are, in many cases, conditioned from childhood abuse to go on to accept this abuse later in life.

Narcissistic parents can do a lot of damage to empathic children. If you were raised by a narcissist, you may have many of the more damaging qualities of your Empathic gift amplified. For that reason, you may often feel like you are cursed rather than gifted. For empathic children raised by narcissistic parents, it is not unusual to have virtually zero boundaries, an excessive need to please others, and an inability to put yourself first. These are already things that Empaths struggle with, and they are amplified through the trauma and abuse incurred through narcissistic-to-victim relationships. If you have experienced this type of trauma in your childhood and have not yet sought support, you may consider doing so now. Doing so will support you in unraveling the abuse symptoms, as well as in working toward empowering you to feel more confident and strong in your gift of being an Empath. With the right support and healing, you can begin using your empathic gift for good, instead of feeling bound to your abuser through it.

Parenting as An Empath

Later in your life, you may choose to have children. If you do, being an Empath and a parent can be somewhat challenging. The connection we have to our children biologically further enhances the Empathic connection that we have toward them. This means that we feel toward them infinitely deeper than we already feel toward others. If you are an Empath and understand how complex this already is, you can imagine how much more intense it can be with children.

As a parent who is also an Empath, it can sometimes be challenging to raise your children. With so much information out there about what is right and what is wrong, it can be easy to quickly feel overwhelmed and like you are making severe mistakes just for the average person. Add in

49

the Empathic tendencies and it can become downright terrifying. Furthermore, you are more likely to give in to your children and teach them things such as having weak boundaries or taking advantage of other people because you are continually trying to meet their every need. Empathic parents have a tendency to avoid punishing or disciplining children in any way, which means it can be a challenge to teach your child right from wrong.

Other things that may happen if you are an Empathic parent include: having all of the other parents confiding in you, feeling overly protective when your children are experiencing adversity, and projecting your own fears and symptoms unto your children. As an Empath, being a parent can be challenging but also wonderful. You *are* raising the next generation to feel supported and cared for so that they can assist in the ascension of society and Earth. However, you are also among some of the earliest generations at this time to be experiencing life as an Empath to this degree, meaning that you yourself may feel very minimal support and that it can be challenging and frustrating at times in ways that non-Empath parents would simply not understand.

When it comes to Empathic parenting, a good system to look into is using positive discipline as well as attachment parenting styles. When you join these forums and pay attention to blogs that revolve around this topic, you can begin to learn how you can honor your Empathic self while still nurturing healthy boundaries and teaching your children important life lessons.

Parenting Empathic Children

If you are an Empath parenting an Empath, you have a lot of benefits to offer. However, it can also come with its own unique challenges. With two Empaths in the house, particularly if one is younger and the other is still learning about their gifts, some of the challenges you may face include having excessive energies in the home, two overly sensitive beings that may not have the tools to cope, and a tendency to escalate each other's symptoms resulting in two extremely overwhelmed individuals. Being the parent, you know it is your duty to calm things down and lead with a level focus. However, being the Empathic parent, you know this is your duty yet you still may struggle to manage your own energies so that you can be readily available for your child's needs as well.

As a parent who is Empathic and who is raising an Empath child, you are in a unique position to offer your child access to resources (namely, you) that you may not have had growing up. This means that the more you educate yourself on being an  Empath and on what it is like growing up, the more support you can provide to your child. While this will not undo all that may have happened to you growing up, it will support you in making sure these things do not happen to your child.

Beyond becoming a resource yourself, it is important to understand that you are still just a parent. You are not intended to be perfect, nor have you ever been expected to be perfect. While you may feel the sting of mistakes deeper than others, realize that you are still entitled to making your mistakes. This is not something that you need to be ashamed of. Own the fact that you are a human and forgive yourself anytime something happens that feels like a "failure." Recognize it as an opportunity to learn and commit to serving and nurturing yourself and your child's needs in a more positive and effective way going forward. Having the support of fellow Empathic mothers and fathers who are also raising Empathic children may be extremely beneficial in this case.

Chapter 6: Empathic Re-Wiring

"Whenever you are on the side of the majority, it is time to pause and reflect."
- *Mark Twain*

If you have been raised in a way that damaged your Empathic abilities and lead to you feeling ashamed about yourself and your gifts, you will likely need to do some Empathic re-wiring. These re-wiring practices will support you in removing the idea that you are damaged or fundamentally "wrong" and will provide you with the ability to regain your position as an empowered Empath. For those who have been raised in abusive or neglectful households that failed to recognize and support your Empathic tendencies, these practices are essential in supporting your ability to heal the wounded healer archetype and regain empowerment and confidence!

Dealing with Low Self-Esteem

As an Empath likely raised by a house that was not understanding of Empaths, your belief system has probably been wired in a way that reduced your self-esteem. Because you were not well-understood growing up, a lot of the beliefs you gained from family, friends, and society itself may have insinuated that you were "broken" and that you needed fixing. In other words, they did not understand you, they were intimidated by your differences, and they wanted to break you down and make you more "normal." This can lead to low self-esteem as a result of not feeling confident in your ability to express yourself as who you are. You may have even learned to express yourself in a way that is not accurate to who you truly are, causing you to feel dissociated from your own identity. If this happened in adolescence when you were in the process of discovering your identity, this could be particularly damaging to your self-esteem.

The best way to regain your self-esteem and increase your confidence levels can be done through a number of ways. The first step is becoming aware of your truth and knowing who you are. If you have made it this far into the book, you have already made step one. If you are just discovering this information for the first time it may take a while to sink in, but once you have developed an understanding of who you are, you can begin to make sense of everything (including your past) and progress to the next steps to improving your self-esteem and becoming a confident Empath. The following practices in this chapter will be extremely beneficial for you.

Unwiring Every Negative Belief You Picked Up

One of the first steps in rewiring yourself is unwiring every negative belief you have picked up throughout your life. This means disassembling your belief systems and replacing them with true, empowering beliefs. This is not an easy task and takes time replacing old beliefs with more empowering beliefs. Once accomplished, it allows you to step into a better reality and live life from your own perspective, as opposed to living a life with clouded judgments influenced by other people's negative beliefs.

To begin the unwiring process, challenge, and question *everything.* Every time you begin behaving as a result of a specific belief you have, question it. Ask yourself where that belief came from and if it truly is yours. If not, begin the process of replacing the old negative belief with your true empowering belief by first identifying the new belief, then reinforcing it by using positive affirmations, visualization, and goal setting. (*See: Using Positive Reinforcement and Motivation.*)

It is important to understand that when you are in the process of unwiring your beliefs to later rewire them with your true beliefs, you must make sure that you are not choosing your beliefs based on popular thinking or opinion. You are your own person, and you are entitled to have your own beliefs, even if they are against popular opinion. Unpopular beliefs are a reality of life and, when they are being honest, virtually everyone will admit that they have a handful of unpopular beliefs. Just because we do not tend to talk about them as often does not mean they still exist. Use your intuition when choosing what beliefs to instill. The beliefs that resonate with you and make you feel aligned to who you are will be the most beneficial.

It is important that you do not endure the entire unwiring and rewiring process only to find yourself coming out the other side with more beliefs that are not true to who you are. This can be a challenge, especially if you are facing low self-esteem and low self-confidence from your conditioning and upbringing, but it is important. Take your time and make sure that as you undergo this process, you also give yourself the space to heal. Healing each layer as you peel it back is an important part of the process. As you heal, you give yourself permission to fully unwire and release all of these negative beliefs and replace them with your own true empowering beliefs, popularity aside.

As you continue to go through this process, you will likely find that there are far more beliefs to be replaced than you initially thought there would be. Since you are an Empath, you have been absorbing beliefs your entire life, whether they were yours or not. As children, we naturally take on the beliefs of our peers and our authorities in society. However, as Empathic children, we take them even further. You may hear one thing one time, and it instantly creates a belief within you, especially if you heard it in childhood. For example, if in the middle of a fight with a parent they told you "you are unlovable." Alternatively, if you hear something repeated to you constantly throughout your life, you can adopt that as a belief as well. For example, in the midst of being bullied, someone may have told you something like "you suck," "you are too fat," "no one likes you," etc. Because of the pain that inflicted, it resonated deep within you and may have become a genuine belief of yours.

Realize that rationality has very little to do with the initial formation of beliefs, especially in childhood. Even if you rationally knew that the belief was wrong or false, you likely still held onto it anyway. This means that as you go along, you will need to honor yourself even when it does not make sense as to why irrational beliefs seem to have such a stronghold in your mind. Instead, give yourself space and recognize that a large part of this rewiring process is healing the beliefs, no matter where they come from. Let yourself release them so that in their place you can input your true beliefs, thus giving you freedom from the false negative beliefs you have been holding onto and allowing you to live a life aligned with your true positive beliefs that serve you.

Rewiring with Positive Beliefs and Intentions

Positive beliefs and intentions are any beliefs and intentions that genuinely align with your best interest. These positive beliefs and intentions can often be contradicted by uninspiring, negative beliefs you have been fed growing up.

When you are in the process of rewiring, make sure that the beliefs you are rewiring with are positive and genuinely serve your well-being and the well-being of others, as well. You can do this by taking a few moments to consider each new belief that you want to affirm to yourself and implant within you. For example, you may have the belief, "money is bad because it makes people evil" which is not a very empowering or positive belief system. Instead, you may want to reframe your perspective and create a new belief, "I will be wealthy and I choose to be loving in how I use my money."

Now, obviously it is going to take some time to replace the old belief with a more empowering positive belief. To achieve full replacement with the new belief, it needs to be ingrained into your sub-conscious mind. That is how the positive belief will actually have an effect on your life.

In order to ingrain the new empowering, positive belief into your sub-conscious mind, you will need to use the power of *repetition*. This is what the sub-conscious mind responds to. Once something has been repeated enough times, it will become "automatic" or in this case "sub-conscious." Think of it like driving a car. When you first started to learn to drive a car, it was incredibly overwhelming as there were so many things to know all at once. But once you practiced enough times, it eventually became sub-conscious and now when you drive a car, you don't even have to think about all the individual tasks required to drive the car.

There are a few ways we can use *repetition* when it comes to new positive beliefs. We will go through this into greater detail in the next heading, *"Positive Reinforcement to the Sub-Conscious Mind."*

Positive Reinforcement to the Sub-Conscious Mind
There are a few tools we can use for positive reinforcement to the sub-conscious mind. A combination of all these tools used repetitively over time will have astounding effects on instilling your mind with positive, empowering beliefs and thus a much better and happier life. These tools include:

Positive Visualization
You might not have experienced it yet, but Empaths have great potential to be creative. Positive Visualization can be a great way to use that creativity you contain and is also a great tool to support your mind in genuinely being able to see a positive future. It gets your mind working and starts the manifestation process. Imagine the ideal situation you'd like to be in a few years from now. Where is that place for you? What does it sound like? Who are the people around you? What do you look like? How do you feel? What luxuries are there? For many, visualizing positive things happening for them is a challenge. If you can begin to practice incorporating positive visualization into your daily life, it becomes easier and easier for you to see, believe and work towards what you desire to have. Then, it becomes easier for you to actually have it. Pick a time of the day that best suits you to do some positive visualization.

Positive Affirmations
Positive Affirmations are a great tool to add to visualization because they support you in having a positive, can-do attitude toward achieving your goals. It can be very powerful to start writing, reciting and listening to positive affirmations of things you would like to be or have in your life. When repeated on a daily basis, it will start to mold your mind and perspective towards positivity. Examples of some

empowering positive affirmations include:

- I have the power to create change
- I forgive myself for my past
- I am worthy of love and joy
- I am worthy of a fantastic life
- I am a creative being
- Positivity is a choice I choose to make everyday
- I choose to be happy and completely love myself today
- I am becoming a better version of myself each and everyday
- Beautiful things happen to me
- I do not seek approval from anyone. I am enough
- I only surround myself with positive and encouraging people
- I am deserving of an abundant lifestyle
- I am successful
- I take responsibility for my successes and failures
- I will accept nothing but the best
- New opportunities come easily to me
- Positive energy surrounds me
- I set clear goals and work to complete them everyday

Goal Setting
Goal Setting is incredibly important because it takes your dreams and desires into account and gives you a real focus toward achieving them and bringing them into your reality. There is something incredibly powerful about writing down your goals. By writing a goal down that you want to achieve in the future allows the goal to become more real in the mind. Once the goal has been written down it becomes easier to break the goal down into smaller goals in order to achieve the desired goal. Another benefit of writing down your goals is it allows you to be reminded of the goal every day and remain focused. Something like a whiteboard can be a great addition to your bedroom so you can see your goals every day when you wake up. Add some pictures or photos next to these goals for more motivation. Make it become more real in the mind.

To-do Lists
To-do lists are a great addition to goal setting. When we set out to achieve big goals (that could take months to a year to achieve), what can often occur after a few weeks is we can feel we have not made any or very minimal progress and it can become easy to feel demotivated. To-do lists are a great solution to this. When we desire to achieve a big goal, we need to break that goal down into many smaller steps. Steps that can be done on a daily basis. These steps need to be written down in our To-do list and when we complete each specific task we can cross it off which is going to give us that beautiful feeling of accomplishment and progression. We will start to feel like we are getting closer to our goal one step at a time thus making us feel even more motivated. When we don't have that To-do list it can become easy to forget about all the progress we have made and focus on how much more we still have to go.

A free website I like to use for my To-do list is; www.todoist.com It enables you to add and cross off all your tasks very easily.

Appreciation and Gratitude Journals
The 4 tools I have previously mentioned are all great tools for your mind to focus on a better future. This particular tool, Appreciation and Gratitude Journals are a great tool to pause and reflect on the present moment and recognize all the things you are grateful for. It can become very easy to get caught up in the future which can leave us unsatisfied at times because we are always wanting more. It's important to stop and take the time to appreciate what we have in life.

The powerful thing about taking the time to recognize what you are appreciative for and writing this down in your gratitude journal, is that you actually increase your vibration and you will naturally attract more things in the future to be grateful for. Crazy right?

It can also be an effective method to shift your perspective when you feel like you 'have the world on your shoulders' and things aren't actually that bad. Another way I like to practice my appreciation is when I have a 'little win' or some beneficial event occurs for the day, I will take a moment to stop and give my gratitude to the Universe. You will be surprised how much this tool will benefit your life.

All of these five tools will work best collectively to encourage you, motivate you, give you hope, improve your self-esteem, and inspire you to keep pushing in a positive direction.

Consuming Positive Self-Development Material
Another great way to rewire your brain is to continually consume positive self-development material. Reading and listening to materials that are designed to inform you about new perspectives, share opinions with you, and support you in rewiring your brain to a more positive mindset are all extremely powerful in unwiring your brain from negative conditioning you received growing up.

It will be especially beneficial if you consume content that is specific to Empaths, as they will be more mindful of how you actually experience the world around you. This type of material can serve you by educating your mind and rewiring your subconscious to let go of beliefs that no longer serve you and replace them with beliefs that will empower you, build your self-esteem and self-confidence, and support you in using your Empathic gift for wonderful things.

I personally love audiobooks. They allow me to consume the information much faster and I can multi-task while listening to the audiobook. Whether that be driving in the car, cleaning the house or walking on the treadmill.

Get Away from the Noise – Live by Yourself
When you are seeking to rewire your brain, it is important to give yourself the space to discover who you truly are and learn what you want to learn. One of the best ways of doing this is living on your own

at least for a while. This gives you a chance to be completely alone and experience who you truly are, free of the pressure of anyone else in your life. It is also a great way to rid yourself of any bad, negative energy that you might have been absorbing.

If you are unable to live alone because you already have a family or you are under conditions where you have to live with other people, consider spending a significant amount of time on your own. Schedule regular breaks and times to be completely by yourself. While this won't be exactly the same, it will give you the opportunity to hear yourself think and figure out what you like to do when you are by yourself. This can support you in having a deeper understanding of who you are, and therefore a greater confidence in expressing yourself.

Even if you can travel somewhere for a period of time by yourself, I would highly recommend this. Get away from the noise and hear yourself think. Take the time to reflect.

Putting Yourself First

Empaths are known for struggling to put themselves first, no matter what the situation is. Many will continue to put others first even long after they begin paying the physical, mental, and emotional price for this behavior. This is a significant symptom of the wounded healer.

As Christopher Walken said, "When you naturally have a healing aura, you attract a lot of damaged people, and having them in your life could drain your energy to the max. A reminder that it is not your job to heal everyone you encounter. You can't pour from an empty cup. Take care of yourself first." Putting yourself first is one of the most selfless things you can do. If you truly want to support other people, putting yourself first and taking care of yourself with the highest quality of care and compassion will support you in being mentally, emotionally, and physically available to support yourself and others for a long time. Treasure yourself in every way possible, and always put yourself first. Be willing to say no, and practice setting boundaries so that you do not deplete your own energy in favor of someone else's needs. Stop tolerating bad energy and negative people.

Surrounding Yourself with The Right Energy

As Jim Rohn said, "You are the average of the five people you spend the most time with." Simply put, energy is contagious. If you are spending time around people with negative energy and are regularly reinforcing negative beliefs around you, you are going to feel an integration of negative energy and beliefs in your own life. Even the most experienced Empaths who have been masterfully protecting themselves and their energy for years find themselves adopting the negative energy and beliefs of those they are around, especially on a regular basis. With Empaths, the people we are emotionally close to seem to have the ability to penetrate through our protection. Although we can work harder to create protection that is impenetrable, consistent exposure can lead to "leaks." Think of it like having constant pressure on the other side of your bubble. Eventually, no matter how hard you try, the bubble can and will burst. If you spend too much time around negative energy and negative beliefs, it will affect you no matter what. It is best to focus on surrounding yourself with the right positive energy rather than trying to fight the negative energy.

Spending majority of your time around people who you can share a positive and healthy relationship with is very important. This does not necessarily mean that you need to discard your old friends and those who you hung out with most. Rather, it simply means spending less time with them in favor of spending more time with people who help you feel great. When you spend time with people who have a positive energy and a set of positive beliefs, you begin to foster these in the same way that you would with negative energy and beliefs. This means that you can begin to experience greater joy in your life. For many Empaths, surrounding themselves with the right group of friends can feel like they are finally coming home to the family they always wanted. It can truly be life changing.

If you are unsure as to how to find a tribe of friends who will be this positive influence in your life, turning to the internet tends to be a great way to start. Beginning too many friendships in search of "the right ones" can be challenging and exhausting, especially for Empaths. Giving yourself the opportunity to meet people online first and get to know them more before building a true relationship with them can be a

61

powerful way to get to know new friends. You can also begin spending more time in areas where more spiritual people hangout. Metaphysical and folk festivals tend to be filled with people who are more Empathic, allowing you to have access to a wealth of new people you can begin hanging out with. There, you may just meet the friends that will change your life. This could be something that you could add to your positive affirmations. I also want to note that as you become a better version of yourself over time and increase your vibration, naturally, you will start to attract higher quality people into your life.

Meeting new friends, especially in person, may be a great way for you to begin using your gift as well. Try relaxing your mind and starting from "neutral" when you are making new friends. Then, allow yourself to read their energy using your gift. Consider what knowingness comes through for you. If it is positive and resonates, there is a good chance that the friendship will become a great one. If it is negative or feels misaligned, then you know that you do not need to invest too much time in building that relationship because it likely will not become fulfilling for either of you in the end.

Chapter 7: Empath Strengths

"The opposite of anger is not calmness, it's empathy."
- *Mehmet Oz*

Empaths have a great deal of strengths that support them in living complete, wonderful lives. When you begin to come to terms with your identity as an Empath and you integrate protection and self-care measures into your life, working in alignment with your empathic gift will become easier. This means that you can begin to enjoy the many benefits and strengths of being an Empath.

Here are some of the wonderful strengths you can look forward to developing and embodying when you awaken to your empathic abilities and begin to take control over them:

A Great Power

Empaths are extremely powerful. This is one of the reasons society puts them down so much. They are afraid of their power. As an individual who can sense things about people that they may not be willing to share, or who can deeply connect to plants and animals around them, you possess clear differences from the average person. In modern society, there are a lot of individuals who are deeply disconnected from the world around them. They struggle to tune in on basic levels, never mind as deeply as you do. You may see it as a weakness, but that is only because you have been conditioned to. In reality, you possess a great power. Once you learn to embrace it and use it to your advantage, you will be unstoppable in creating positive change in the world.

An Amazing Friend

Anyone who has an Empath as a friend should be incredibly grateful. Empaths are amazing friends. Empaths truly cherish the people they love in their life and will go to extreme lengths to help and protect them. They give great advice to their friends. When a friend has a problem or some sort of difficulty, Empaths are happy to use their beautiful gift of empathizing and putting themselves in their friend's shoes to understand the particular situation and figure out what the best possible decision is.

Ability to Detect Red Flags

Because of your ability to see what is going on beneath the surface, you have an uncanny ability to detect red flags in any person or situation. You do this by empathizing with the other person, essentially allowing you to step into their shoes. This means that you can detect the harmony between the person's words, actions and feelings. There, you can determine whether they are acting in alignment with the truth or if they are lying or being dishonest in any way. By sensing any signs of incongruence, you are able to detect possible ulterior motives.

Whether or not you choose to actually recognize and act on these is a completely different story, but your ability to detect them and become aware of them is extremely powerful. You are capable of knowing any time there is something inherently wrong about a situation, making it easy for you to avoid danger and energetic attacks if you are tuned in and capable of acting on this information. If you are not yet, do not worry. As an Empath, you are capable of tapping into this ability at any time. It is not too late for you.

Detecting Compulsive Liars

Another great ability you have with being able to tell what is truly going on under the surface of others is that you can easily detect compulsive liars. When people are lying, you know it almost instantly. Just like the red flags, you can detect the harmony between the person's words, actions and feelings. By recognizing any signs of disharmony, it can be easy for you to suspect lying. This often comes as just a "knowingness" within. This encourages you to refrain from believing them and can support you in preventing yourself from getting drawn in and trapped in their web of lies. The more you practice this, the better you will become at using this gift.

If you are a wounded healer and not able to utilize your gift efficiently, you may find yourself getting trapped into a person's web of lies. This is something important to address in the process of healing this archetype, if you have it.

Strong Creative Talents

Individuals who are gifted Empaths are known to be very strong in their creative talents. As we have already discussed, they are skilled artists, singers, poets, writers and creators in general. Empaths view the  world in a poetic way that enables them to create unique art pieces that highlight their unique view on the world. Their ability to visualize something in their head and bring it into the material world with their creativity is simply amazing. The challenge for most Empaths is first eliminating all the negativity they have absorbed growing up. This negativity could be in the form of doubt, insecurity, fear of failure, and lack of confidence.

Virtually every Empath has the potential to be creative, though how they express or use the trait may vary. In other words, not every Empath will be great at the same thing, but they all will have some degree of creativity that they can use to express themselves and serve the world. This is incredibly satisfying and fulfilling for the Empath.

Excellent Problem Solvers

When an Empath has developed their empathic gift, they can be excellent problem solvers. Using their empathetic ability, they are able to analyze the wants and needs of different parties from multiple points of view. By being able to analyze a certain situation and see many different points of view, gives the Empath a great edge to be able to come up with the best possible solution that will be beneficial for both parties.

Great Entrepreneurship Abilities

Because of their intuitive abilities and their superb ability to solve problems, Empaths make great entrepreneurs. They are highly focused on delivering the best results to their clients, no matter what their line of work may be. Furthermore, they are heavily driven by a desire to have freedom and to escape from the toxic, overwhelming, and greedy environments of traditional 9 - 5 jobs.

Empath entrepreneurs are great at coming up with creative companies that reach the needs of their clients in ways that larger companies tend to overlook completely. They typically find themselves in their own companies that offer some form of healing or shifting modern society. Counselors, life and business coaches, alternative healers, artists, writers, and other career paths are extremely common for Empaths to choose. Fortunately, each of these can be done on an entrepreneurial basis. They are also excellent choices as they cater to the unique strengths and weaknesses of the Empath, allowing them to shine their brightest and serve in the way that their soul needs to shine.

If you are an Empath and you are not presently on the path of being an entrepreneur, you may find great joy and benefit in beginning this life path. With your gifts and abilities, you have the capacity to begin your life as an entrepreneur and create great success in doing so. There are many great benefits to choosing this career path. Some of these benefits include:

- You are able to experience much more flexibility and freedom in your life compared to working a job
- You can control your own working schedule and holidays
- You do not have to deal with the draining and toxic environments of a 9-5 job
- You can choose the people you want to work with or work solely online
- You can work from home
- You have the potential to earn much more than what a job can offer you
- You can put your creative ability to good use
- Become more fulfilled and happy in what you do
- More travel opportunities may present themselves to you

- General health and happiness will improve when you remove yourself from negative, toxic work environments

Many people believe that empathic entrepreneurship is the way of the future. As more and more people seek to lead a more socially conscious and responsible life, many are avoiding large businesses and corporations that are typically known for being irresponsible, unkind, and savage in their business dealings. These exact same people are seeking entrepreneurs running their own socially responsible businesses in a way that genuinely serves their needs on a personal level. As an Empath, you have exactly what it takes to serve in this way, meaning that you and your gifts are exactly what these people are looking for.

Strong Relation to Animals and Plants

Another great strength possessed by Empaths is their connection to animals and plants. As you know from animal Empaths and plant Empaths, these individuals have incredible talents when it comes to communicating with animals and plants. This is a breath of fresh air in a world where very little concern has been shown to the environment and those who inhabit it. Many humans in the modern world rarely consider other humans, let alone other species or life forms. As an Empath, you may have a powerful ability to relate to these life forms and protect them from the destruction of humans who experience little to no empathy in their lives.

Animals and plants are also believed to be Empathic, meaning that you may find that animals and plants respond well to you, also. You may find yourself attracting animals into your life and having an uncanny ability to help plants thrive in a way that others may struggle to do. This is because they are intuitive and can sense that you are kind. This allows them to automatically trust in you and feel safe, protected and nourished in your presence. They sense your energy, and it supports them in thriving.

Chapter 8: Empath Weaknesses

"We are a slave to our emotions when we don't acknowledge or fear their teachings – be brave through empathy."
- *Christel Broederlow*

As with anything, Empaths also have weaknesses. The weaknesses you face may be debilitating for you, depending on how much you experience them. Unfortunately, most Empaths are not aware of what they are so they end up going through life living in fear of their weaknesses. This prevents them from developing their strengths and can result in them feeling overburdened by their gift. Trust that if you recognize or relate to any of these weaknesses, recognizing them and giving yourself the space to come to terms with them is important. This is where you can begin to heal them and step into your power. As a result, you can keep your weaknesses in check as you give yourself the space required to develop your strengths. Then, a natural balance will arise, and you will have the opportunity to live a life in alignment with your gift.

Attracting Narcissistic People

One unfortunate weakness of Empaths, even stronger ones, is attracting narcissistic people into their lives. Although you might feel intolerant toward narcissists, you may also find yourself overly surrounded by them. The reason why this happens is simple: you have the one thing they lack. Empathy.

Narcissists are drawn to people who have excess empathy because they can exploit that empathy to get what they want. They also love people who have a low sense of self-worth and low self-esteem. If you are not careful, they can exploit you to have their own selfish needs met. This can result in Empaths finding themselves trapped in narcissistic relationships that drain them of their energy and cause them to feel overwhelmed and taken advantage of. Unfortunately, because you can see from the other person's perspective and many narcissists are believed to be narcissistic as a result of childhood trauma, this can result in you siding with the narcissist. Your desire to heal others may result in you attempting to save someone who cannot be saved. That is unless they choose to save themselves.

If you find yourself being surrounded by narcissists or recognize narcissistic relationships presently or previously in your life, this is likely because of the fact that you are Empathic. When not properly protected, you can easily be disillusioned by narcissists who can result in a lot of trauma in your own life. If you *are* presently in a toxic relationship with a narcissist, my book: *"Emotional and Narcissistic Abuse: The Complete Survival Guide to Understanding Narcissism, Escaping the Narcissist in a Toxic Relationship Forever, and Your Road to Recovery,"* may be the answer for you. This book can support you in understanding the nature of the abuse and finding a safe way to free yourself from it in a way that is compassionate and nurturing toward your unique empathic needs.

It is important to understand that even if you are finding yourself surrounded by narcissists, there is a way to protect yourself and you are not doomed to being abused and hurt by narcissists for your entire life. As you strengthen your protection abilities, self-worth, self-care and heal from your mistrust in yourself and your inner voice, you will begin to find it easier for you to identify and recognize a narcissist. Then, you can avoid them in favor of healthier relationships.

Knowing Better but Not Doing Better

Empaths have a tendency to know better but not actually do better. This is not because they don't want to do better, but because they are conditioned to think of themselves as "wrong." Through bullying, societal conditioning, and other abandonment in childhood and young adulthood, Empaths are taught that their inner knowingness is false and that they should not believe it. This causes doubt in the Empaths intuition. If this has happened to you, you might find it difficult to trust and act on your inner knowingness. As a result, you may find yourself missing out on opportunities or kicking yourself for not acting sooner. This is extremely common. Feeling like you should have acted sooner because "you knew better" is a really common feeling for Empaths.

It is important to note that until now, even if you *did* know better, you didn't do better because you genuinely couldn't. Your conditioning resulted in you feeling and believing that you were truly unable to act on what you felt you knew. As a result, you did not act. This is not your fault. If this is something you face, healing your trust in yourself, your intuition and strengthening your sense of self-worth and self-confidence will help you in believing your gut reaction and feeling confident in your inner knowingness. Then, you can begin knowing and doing better. As a result, you will feel like you are living in greater alignment with yourself and you will have fewer instances of feeling like "I shouldn't have done that!" or "I should have done this!"

Taking on Responsibilities that Aren't Yours

As an Empath, you may find yourself taking on responsibilities that are not yours. Empaths have a sense of duty that is hard for them to avoid. Knowing things on a deeper level leads to you feeling like it is your responsibility to do the things that others are not doing. This is because you feel that if you don't, no one will. As a result, you may find yourself struggling to balance too many responsibilities, many of which are not rightfully yours. Many Empaths report feeling like they are "carrying the weight of the world on their shoulders" when they experience these symptoms.

Taking on these responsibilities can manifest on a personal level, a collective level, or both. You may find yourself taking on other people's responsibilities directly in your life. For example, at work, you may realize that people are not doing their complete jobs because of personal struggles. As a result, you take on their responsibilities for them. This can be kind, but it can also lead to you being overwhelmed and taken advantage of. You may also find this happening in other areas of your life as well. Many Empaths take on the responsibilities of others and become taken advantage of, by anyone from friends and family, to coworkers and even parents of other children if you are a parent yourself. It is important to realize that you still need to put yourself first. Helping people is great but you still need to keep a balance in your life and establish healthy boundaries. We will go into more detail about this in the next chapter.

On a collective level, Empaths may take on more responsibility by feeling like it is their duty to heal the world of major tragedies. For example, you may find yourself feeling as though you are personally responsible for healing world hunger, ending war, or finding homes for the homeless. This can result in a constant sense of feeling unfulfilled because no one person can heal these ailments in the world.

Struggling to Live a "Normal" Life

Many Empaths struggle to live a "normal" life. Because of how pain has integrated itself into everyday life and into the conditioning of society, many Empaths find themselves resenting normal life on every level. Still, they may also find themselves longing to live one. This can create inner conflict for any Empath. On one hand, leading a life numb to pain and filled with misery is unbearable. On the other hand, you may find yourself just wanting to fit in. It may feel like you have *never* fit in and you may blame your inability to be "normal" for the reason why you feel as though you never fit in. This can result in you feeling the inner conflict.

As an Empath, going to a mundane job that you dislike filled with people who are plagued by negative energy can be nonsensical and depressing. You may find yourself struggling to assimilate into this standard life. You may even become physically, mentally, and emotionally sick from trying to live this lifestyle. For many, there seems to be no alternative. This is why a growing majority of Empaths are choosing the entrepreneur path. Not only does it provide freedom from these soul-sucking experiences, but it also gives the Empath an opportunity to do something that truly has meaning for them.

The feeling of struggle does not end with career, either. Many Empaths struggle to perform everyday activities such as going shopping, spending extended amount of time with friends or family, or even watching certain things on TV or scrolling through social media. Because of their heightened sensitivities, this can be truly draining and overwhelming for an Empath.

71

Difficulty with Routines

Empaths and routines are typically not something that mixes well. Empaths tend to find themselves struggling to deal with routines. As you may recall, Empaths feel things deeply and intensely. Often, this leads to an Empath always looking to have some sense of feeling that creates a deep sense of fulfillment.

You may find that you struggle to create routine in your life and that staying aligned with a routine for any length of time is virtually impossible. You crave spontaneity, mystery, and change. In there, you find feelings that you love to explore and enjoy. This results in you feeling fulfilled and alive. For you, routine may create numbness and a lack of emotional fulfillment. Finding ways to be spontaneous is a great way to ensure that you live your best life.

Weak Boundaries

Empaths are known to have weak boundaries, especially early in their development. Your ability to feel people deeply results in you regularly giving people the benefit of the doubt, often stepping into a dangerous cycle of allowing them to take advantage of you over and over again. This can be traumatic for Empaths who do not realize that they cannot save someone who has no desire to help themselves. You may have even been conditioned to abandon your boundaries from a young age, further weakening your boundaries. If this is the case, then you may already be aware of the symptoms you experience in your life as a result of weak boundaries.

Weak boundaries can also occur from a low sense of self-worth and self-esteem which is common in Empaths. When you do not value yourself highly as an individual, you are more likely to tolerate toxic people and toxic environments. Having strong boundaries is all about saying "No!" more often and having no tolerance for anyone treating you wrongfully. Remove yourself from people and environments that do not have a positive impact on your life. As you work to increase your sense of self-worth and self-esteem and respect yourself more, you will naturally develop stronger boundaries.

Tendency to Have Addictions

If you are not adequately supported in your empathic gifts, you may feel drawn toward having addictions to support you in numbing out the pain and "trying to fit in." Many Empaths are reported to have "addictive personalities" because of this. It is important to understand that this behavior in an Empath is often rooted in a desire to relieve themselves of the pain that comes from feeling other's pain so deeply. This can add to the complexity of the addictions, meaning it is important to seek professional assistance in relieving these addictions should you find yourself facing them. Finding professional support that understands Empaths can be extra helpful, although it may be more challenging to find. When trying to remove an addiction, I would recommend replacing the particular addiction with something else in your life that is going to have a positive impact on your life. This could range from training at the gym, playing a team sport, learning how to dance, learning how to play a musical instrument or starting your own business.

Chapter 9: Empathic Protection

"When I peeled back the layers, I found a beautiful resilience inside. This is how I know I will always thrive."
- *Lori Schaffer*

One of the biggest reasons why being an Empath can be considered a "curse" is because many people are not educated in how they can protect themselves from the harsher symptoms, such as carrying too many energies, stepping into someone's experience without being able to step back out, or not knowing how to refrain from stepping in overall. Knowing how to protect yourself can have a powerful impact on empowering you to elevate from the wounded healer to the empowered Empath. Here is what you need to do.

Recognize Red Flags and Walk Away

One of the gifts of being an Empath is that you can quickly detect red flags in situations or people. It is easy for you to identify compulsive behaviors such as lying, exploiting others, or otherwise being abusive or negative toward those around you. Being an Empath means that you can identify these and can then walk away. For some Empaths, the walking away part is particularly challenging. If this is you, learning to walk away is important.

Walking away from situations that do not serve you is not selfish. Many Empaths mistakenly believe that they need to "save" other people. This leads to them getting caught in situations where they perpetually feel responsible for someone else, despite this not being true. Your gifts were not given to you so that you could live in a world of abuse and experience direct damage as a result. They were given to you so that you can save the world. That is likely why you get caught up in your desire to save individual people: it is your nature to "save." However, many Empaths are not taught to understand what this actually means.

74

You come here to save the planet from a lack of empathy and compassion, but not with the personal responsibility to take on the energy of every individual you meet. Instead, you can help by empowering, uplifting, and inspiring other people to do better in their lives. Those who desire to do better will follow your example and find themselves being saved *by themselves.* You are not here to save them: you are here to show them how to save themselves. This means that your only responsibility is to save *yourself* and lead by example. Through this, you will inspire others to do the same.

Recognize and Protect Yourself from Energy Vampires

Energy vampires are people who can drain a great deal of energy from you. They tend to have problem after problem, and they constantly come to you, asking for more than a reasonable amount of support. As an Empath, you feel into their position, empathize with them, and find yourself feeling personally responsible for providing them with the energy required to do what is needed from you. This quickly turns into a treadmill, where you are constantly running to meet the energy needs of the person but you are never able to fulfill their needs. This is because they are an energy vampire.

In order to protect yourself from energy vampires, you need to teach yourself how to say "no." Learning to say no and stand behind it is important. This is how you can support yourself in feeling confident and protected in saying no. When you say no to an energy vampire, make sure that you consciously say no with your energy as well. Some people will envision their protective shield blocking out the request, preventing the energy from coming into their space altogether. Keeping out the energy of the energy vampire is important. If you let it in, it can begin to create empathic sensations within you that might cause you to change your mind. This is less of a worry when you become stronger in protecting yourself, but early on you are susceptible to changing your mind as a result of this energy.

Recognizing energy vampires and learning how to say no to them will also require you to protect yourself from shouldering any further responsibility. Affirming to yourself that it is not your duty to fulfill other people's needs beyond what you feel is reasonable is important. If you are not doing it out of love for yourself and the other person, you are not doing it for the right person. If you are doing something that extends more of your energy than you can reasonably give, then you are giving too much. Make sure that you educate yourself on saying no and that you consciously clear your energy field from the request as well. This will protect you against the energy, the request, and the energy vampire. You also want to minimize the amount of time you spend around the energy vampire as much as possible and practice setting stronger boundaries with them in regards to what you are willing to listen to and engage with in order to create a stronger sense of protection against the energy vampire. This way, you do not feel like you are constantly in protection mode and you give yourself space to breathe and enjoy life.

Save Yourself from Time Vampires Too
In addition to energy vampires, there are also time vampires. Frequently, an energy vampire may also be a time vampire. However, not all time vampires are energy vampires. Time vampires are people who take up far too much of your time. You may find yourself constantly doing things for them, spending excessive time with them, or investing a great deal of time worrying about them. As a result, they end up taking up far too much of your precious time.

The best way to deal with a time vampire is to limit the time that you are willing to share with them. Decide what your boundary needs to be, set it, and stand behind it. Begin reinforcing it by only giving them the allotted amount of time and then saying no when the boundary is reached. This also counts when you are thinking about them. If you find yourself worrying about the person, say no to yourself and set a boundary with yourself as well. Reducing the amount of time you are willing to spend on a person, especially one that is toxic toward you (whether consciously or unconsciously) can support and protect you.

Even though it is nice to help people and you want to help others feel good in their lives, it is not your responsibility. Have an honest conversation with yourself about why you feel personally responsible for others and then begin to enforce boundaries with yourself as well. Creating these personal boundaries will make it easier for you to prevent yourself from feeling personally responsible for everyone else's needs and feelings. Then, it will become easier for you to say no and protect your time. When you do say no, make sure that you fulfill that time instead with something that is a genuine act of self-love. The more you take good care of yourself, the easier it is to understand why you deserve your time, energy, and attention even more than anyone else. Even if that does not feel natural or "right" to you in the beginning. Soon, you will understand that it is a necessary protection *and* self-care practice. Not only does it help you feel great, but it will also amplify your ability to help others.

Preserve and Protect Your Energy

It is important that you learn to preserve and protect your energy as an Empath. Knowing how to "tune out" of the world from time to time to give yourself the space to recharge is important. One great way to do

this is through getting a high-quality set of noise-cancelling headphones and putting them on when you go out in public or when you are in noisy environment. While you may not be able to do this every time, using them in certain circumstances can support you in staying focused on the energy of the music rather than the

environment around you. Consider using music that is uplifting and upbeat so that it actually amplifies your energy, rather than you going out and coming home feeling depleted.

Another way to protect your energy is to begin practicing energetic boundaries. This means that you make yourself unavailable to tune into the energies of those around you unless you give yourself permission to do so. Set the boundary with yourself that you are not going to tune into any energy.

Learning to switch your gift "on" and "off" can take practice, and the best way to do it is just to start. Soon, you will learn to be firm and consistent, and your boundaries will be effortless to uphold. This means that you begin gaining power and control over your Empath gift so that you no longer feel like you are being ruled by it. Instead, you can rule the gift and use it as you need to in order to support you in your life and soul purpose, as well as in leading a quality life.

Shield Your Aura

Shielding is a powerful practice that Empaths use to protect themselves from external energies. This is a form of creating an energetic boundary that can stay in place and keep you feeling protected without you always having to be consciously working toward it. In the beginning, your energetic shield may need continuous conscious reinforcement. Once you become more skilled with it, however, it becomes a lot easier.

The best shield to consider using when you are going out in public, or anywhere that your gift may be overly activated, is called a bubble shield. This shield is created by you envisioning a white light glowing in your solar plexus. This light then grows and grows, purifying your body and energy field and filling it with white light. Let this light grow until it forms a bubble that extends four feet away from your body in either direction, including down into the Earth. This shield is one that, once built, will stay in place as long as you desire. If you feel that your shield is down or you have taken it down by accident, you can always recreate it using the same strategy. Some people even choose to create a new one every morning to support them in staying protected throughout the day. Any time that you feel your energy is being threatened visualize your shield to reinforce it and keep unwanted energies out.

Leave Abusive Relationships

This can be challenging, but leaving abusive relationships is essential if you want to protect yourself as a human and as an Empath. If you are in an abusive relationship, whether it is with a family member, house-mate, friend, spouse, or coworker, you need to take all measures possible to leave this relationship. These people are robbing you of your valuable energy and you need to do everything you can to protect yourself. Removing yourself completely from these people is the best solution. If you cannot leave the relationship for some reason, say you share custody of a child with your spouse or you cannot leave your job so you have to put up with your coworker, do everything you can to minimize contact to as little as possible. Then, give yourself the space, time, and resources to begin healing from the damage of this relationship.

If you are in a relationship with a narcissistic and abusive spouse, reading my book, *""Emotional and Narcissistic Abuse: The Complete Survival Guide to Understanding Narcissism, Escaping the Narcissist in a Toxic Relationship Forever, and Your Road to Recovery"* will be extremely valuable to you. An important part of leaving relationships includes leaving them safely and seeking appropriate support in healing afterward. That book covers this in more depth.

Abusive relationships have the capacity to destroy an Empath from the inside out. They will destroy you mentally, physically, emotionally, and energetically. All of your gifts will be exploited, causing you to perceive them through jaded eyes. It can also damage your ability to use them as effectively, or as trustingly. Leaving these relationships will give you the space to heal and recover so that you can tap fully back into your gifts and use them to support you, uplift you, and assist you in achieving your goals throughout your life.

Carry Protective Crystals or Amulets
Something many Empaths do is carry protective crystals and amulets with them when they go out and about. Crystals come in many different varieties, each with unique purposes and abilities to support and protect your energies. Some of the most common ones for Empaths include:

- Amethyst: protects against anxiety and addictive behaviors.
- Obsidian: protects your aura against negative energy.
- Malachite: purifies your energy and promotes a cleaner and more free-flowing aura.
- Lepidolite: supports emotional healing and balance.
- Hematite: absorbs negative energy and calms stress in the body and mind.

Amulets are small ornaments or pieces of jewelry that are believed to protect against danger, evil, or disease. Some Empaths like to purchase these or create their own to wear with them when they go out in public. These support them in feeling confident and protected so that their energy bodies are not attacked or impacted during their daily activities. Depending on what they are made of, they can ward off unwanted energies, prevent you from stepping into and out of other people's energies unintentionally, and prevent you from feeling "blocked" in your energy field.

Chapter 10: Empathic Self-Care

"The deeper your self-love, the greater your protection."
- *Danielle Laporte*

Self-care as an Empath is essential. When you are an Empath, knowing how to rest, recharge, and cleanse your energies can promote a more fluid sense of well-being. These activities can release any energies you may be carrying, as well as produce a greater strength within you so that you can prevent unwanted energies from clinging to you in the first place. Stress and a poor self-care routine can easily result in individuals acquiring unwanted or harmful energies in the first place. So, reducing these and taking care of yourself can minimize the occurrence of this.

Here are some things that you need to begin doing to take care of your energies and keep yourself feeling nourished and supported.

Re-Charge Often
Recharging is an important way to keep your energies full. For an Empath, recharging often happens in nature or through direct rest. When you go into nature, connecting to the elements of the Earth around you can be highly supportive in allowing you to release any unwanted energies and refuel yourself with positive, beneficial energies. Many Empaths report feeling drawn to the forest often, regularly retreating to the forest to find peace and comfort. Some Empaths even recognize the word forest as meaning "for rest."

In addition to relaxing in nature and connecting with the elements, true rest through the form of sleeping can be deeply nourishing for an Empath. You can also spend time with your pets if you have any (which most Empaths do) as they seem to have a deep knowing over how they can support you in feeling nourished and whole. The unconditional love shared between you and your pets is truly nourishing when spending time together.

Many Empaths who are not actively caring for themselves well through recharging frequently will find themselves having disturbed sleep, either not sleeping enough or struggling to stay asleep all-night long. This comes from the chronic stress they are facing. By intentionally creating a stronger sleep routine and getting more sleep, Empaths can support themselves in feeling nourished and recharged so that they can go out and face the next day with confidence and ease.

Exercise Your Creativity

Despite Empaths being highly creative, some will actually shut down their creativity. This may occur from their childhood being abused or bullied around their creative talents, or it may happen occasionally if they are feeling overwhelmed and are struggling to dedicate enough time and attention toward creative outlets.

If you are someone who shuts down your creativity to avoid being bullied or hurt, it is a good idea to begin exploring and exercising your creativity once more. This process can help you awaken your energies again and begin expressing yourself in ways that you have been denying for a long time. Even just starting with something as easy as coloring is a great way to get started. Then, over time, you can move into your preferred mediums of creativity so that you can begin expressing yourself in the ways that feel best to you.

If you are in a funk and it has caused you to refrain from creating recently due to any number of excuses, recognize that the most likely reason is because you are struggling to actually express yourself. For Empaths, artwork is an essential form of self-expression. Naturally, if you stop creating it is important to look into the reason why. Then, you can begin to heal the block and practice creating again. Sometimes, it is as simple as setting aside some time, putting some music on and just doing it.

Consider Working for Yourself

Working for yourself as an Empath can be a powerful form of self-care. Being able to set your own hours and choose your own rules is empowering and can support you in having a positive work environment that enables you to create an income while feeling inspired and empowered to do so. Furthermore, if you feel a deep calling toward something in particular, such as healing or creating, you can create your own business doing just that. This means that not only do you free yourself from the restraints and toxicity of corporate jobs, but you also enable yourself to do what feels the best for you. This can have an even greater impact on your overall health than you may think, so be sure to consider it!

If you cannot leave your job or working for yourself does not seem reasonable at this time, consider going into business for yourself part-time. Even just creating artwork and selling it online or performing healing services here and there can be a great way to exercise your freedom, tap into your gift, and feel like you are gaining the benefits of working for yourself without losing some of the benefits that come with working for someone else.

Practice Energy Clearing Often

Energy clearing is an absolute must. When you are an Empath, energy clearing goes much beyond basic self-care. This is not just about feeling good, but about actually releasing energies that may be preventing you from doing so. Daily energy clearing practices, such as meditation or binaural beats, are extremely important. You should also have stronger antidotes on hand for those times when you feel that you are carrying an excess of energy and you need freedom from it. These "stronger dose medicines" of energy clearing are ones that may take longer, but will have a great impact on supporting your healing.

Meditate

Meditating is a powerful way of supporting yourself in clearing unwanted energies. Meditating for just ten minutes a day has been said to have a strong impact on supporting you in clearing all that you do not desire to carry with you, freeing your mind so that you can experience more peace and joy in the present moment.

If you find meditating to be challenging, you might consider using guided meditations or music to support you in your meditation practice.

Additionally, you may want to start with meditating for just a couple of minutes at a time, then gradually increasing the amount of time you are meditating until you reach ten minutes per day. This can make it easier for you to build this practice and support it in your daily life.

Hot Showers
Hot showers have a great ability to support you in releasing unwanted energies from your body. Using the hot water to cleanse and purify your body while envisioning all of the unwanted energies going down the drain can be very powerful in energy cleansing. Some people also use bath products that are infused with energy-cleansing materials, such as sage, himalayan salt, or various essential oils to support them in releasing energies. You can also find soaps that are infused with crystals that clear energies, too.

Himalayan Salt Baths
Himalayan salt is said to be great for drawing out toxins from the body, supporting you in releasing any energies that may be stored within your body and cells that are preventing you from clearing your energies effectively. If you do not have access to Himalayan salt, Epsom salts, dead sea salts, and Celtic sea salts are also excellent alternatives.

Binaural Beats
Binaural beats are a form of energetic music designed to support you in attuning yourself to certain energy frequencies. They can promote healing and balance, release energies, and support you in attuning you to virtually any frequency you desire. If you are clearing energies, using a binaural beat specific to clearing energies can be valuable. 536Hz and 432Hz are known to be good ones for energy clearing.

Get Energy Healing Done
If you are feeling particularly overloaded and like you need more support in releasing a great deal of energy, having an energy healing done by a healer can be powerful. Getting reiki or another energy clearing method done by a certified practitioner or Shaman can support you in releasing energies by bringing the skilled hand of a practitioner on board to help you. Think of it as a massage for your aura!

Clear Your Chakras

 Chakras are energy meridians within the body that support various types of energies. We typically recognize seven energy chakras within the body: the root chakra by your tail bone, the sacral chakra by your navel, the solar plexus chakra just below your rib cage, your heart chakra in the center of your chest, your throat chakra in the upper part of your throat, your third eye chakra in the center of your forehead, and your crown chakra directly above the crown of your head. Each of these chakras represents a specific type of energy and needs to be balanced in order to maintain a positive energy flow.

Here is a basic cheat sheet to help you understand and balance the chakras:

- Root Chakra: associated with the color red. Grounding, eating deep red foods, walking on the grass bare footed and wearing the color red can support you in balancing this chakra.
- Sacral Chakra: associated with the color orange. Creativity, exercise, eating orange foods, and wearing the color orange can support you in balancing this chakra.
- Solar Plexus Chakra: associated with the color yellow. Building your confidence and self-esteem, reaching goals, eating yellow and citrusy foods, and wearing the color yellow can support you in balancing this chakra.
- Heart Chakra: associated with the color green. Opening your heart, healing your emotional body, and doing things that engage you in the energies of love and compassion, as well as eating green foods and wearing the color green can support you in balancing this chakra.
- Throat Chakra: associated with the color blue. Speaking your truth, confidence in saying what you mean, eating blue foods,

and wearing the color blue can support you in balancing this chakra.

- Third Eye Chakra: associated with the color indigo. Meditations that open your third eye, daydreaming, awakening your Empathic abilities, eating foods that are indigo and wearing the color indigo can support you in balancing this chakra.
- Crown Chakra: associated with the color violet. Praying, meditating, connecting to source, eating foods that are violet and wearing the color violet can support you in balancing this chakra.

In addition to these basic practices, you can also incorporate many other things such as essential oils, yoga, guided meditations, Reiki, and other practices in clearing and balancing these chakra energies.

Practice A Healthy Social Life

Engaging in a healthy social life and practicing positive activities is important for an Empath. Make sure that you are surrounding yourself with the right people who genuinely have your best interest at heart. You should also make sure that they are focused on assisting you in creating your best life possible.

Find and spend time with friends who will enjoy doing activities such as creating, attending positive social events, and engaging in activities such as yoga and meditation with you. While not all of your friends need to have these activities in common with you, having some that are willing to embrace your Empath path with you and join in on these activities can assist you in feeling supported and empowered by your friends.

Make sure that if you do have friends who are not entirely supportive that you minimize your time with them. You might have friends who are not entirely supportive, not because they are abusive but because they simply do not understand and relate. While you do not need to discard these friends, be mindful of how their beliefs and behavior impacts you and make sure that you refrain from spending too much time with them if they are having a negative impact on you. Do regular check ins to make sure that your friends are positive influences in your life and that you feel happy, supported, and empowered around them.

Thanks to the internet, you also have access to many online support forums and groups where you can connect with fellow Empaths around the world. This may even help you link up with local Empaths who understand you and can support each other. Take advantage of the resources available to you and be sure to find people who assist you in living your best life possible. Even if you naturally lean toward introverted tendencies, having a few people who you come out of your shell around and who you genuinely enjoy can be extremely beneficial to your overall wellbeing.

Take Advantage of To Do Lists

Any Empath who has not grown up educated on how to take care of themselves properly may find themselves feeling overwhelmed and even struggling to cope with feeling like a failure. This comes from having a lowered self-esteem and a sense of self-confidence. As such, setting and accomplishing goals can be extremely fulfilling for Empaths. This can also be a great way to bypass the mundaneness of routines and still get everything done.

Creating a to-do list each morning is a great way to provide yourself with a series of mini-goals that you desire to accomplish each day. Then, as you check things off the list, you will begin to feel fulfilled and satisfied. This can support you in having a deep sense of fulfillment, which is essential for Empaths. It can also support you in raising your self-esteem and self-confidence and in feeling more capable of achieving and accomplishing all that you desire to do.

In addition to creating daily to-do lists, it is wise to set weekly and monthly goals as well. These can provide you with larger goals that give you the opportunity to have even greater accomplishment in your life. The more you check off of these lists, the better you will feel. Thus, you will begin to feel far more positive and better about yourself.

This is both a great way to set aside all-day routines while still getting things done, and to feel great. For an Empath, this can even support you in breaking a mood swing or coming out of an energy funk so that you can begin to enjoy life once again.

Have a Gratitude Journal

Gratitude is a powerful energy that can support in recognizing and highlighting the parts of our lives that we love and enjoy. Keeping a gratitude journal can be a great way to support yourself in feeling better and caring for your energy. When you use a gratitude journal, you train your brain to focus on the positive *in addition to* the negative. It also allows you to reframe the negative. It is a great way to begin to see the silver lining and to develop a sense of optimism.

If you have never used a gratitude journal, you can start now by purchasing a journal and committing to writing in it daily or weekly, whatever suits you best. You can journal, brain dump, use bullet points, or otherwise write down what you are grateful for in any way that feels right for you. As long as you are consistent, you will find that it works great and supports you by promoting a more uplifted mood and a general sense of wellbeing. You should also write in your gratitude journal whenever you have a small win or celebratory moment in your life. Even giving thanks to the Universe is a great practice.

The other powerful thing about practicing gratitude is that it re-wires your brain to an appreciative and optimistic perspective. Over time by practicing this skill, you will notice you will have many more things to be grateful for.

Chapter 11: Ascending Earth Consciousness

"Your entire life has unfolded for your heart's ascension to love."
- *Bryant McGill*

We are living in the Aquarian Age: a time where Earth consciousness is being ascended. As a result, many more Empaths are incarnating into the world with the intention of assisting in shifting consciousness and supporting the awakening of others who are ready to ascend.

If you are an Empath who is presently awakening or who is already awakened to your gifts, there is a good chance that you are among the first to awaken with the intention of supporting others who are ready. This time can be a challenge for you since much of Earth is still inhabited by challenging, unkind, and even destructive individuals. It is important that you understand that your task is not to awaken everyone: it is to awaken those who are ready to be awakened. Remember, you awaken them by leading an awakened life, not by taking responsibility for their awakening and forcing it in any way.

At this time in society, we are beginning to recognize our own creative powers and natural talents. We are discovering that we are far beyond and above the very basic and destructive behaviors we have been portraying for many generations. We are ready to begin living a life in alignment with our energetic selves, realizing our fullest potential and living it out as we are here.

Some people who are awakening at this time are having great challenges with the energy. Of those awakening, you know there is so much better and yet it may cause deep aches within you in realizing that they are not. You may feel a lot of pressure to take on a significant amount of energy and "save the world." While that is what you are here to do, you are not here to do it alone. You do not have to take the weight of the entire world on your shoulders.

Because so many Empaths are incarnating at this time, there are large masses of Empaths prepared to work together toward the same goal: ascending Earth energies. This means that you can connect with other Empaths and work together with a group, rather than attempting to do it all yourself and exposing yourself to the massive amount of stress that this task would bring with it.

As an Empath, you may be noticing increasing energies lately. These energies are impacting all of Earth in the ascension of the collective and Earth itself. These symptoms may include things such as mysterious headaches, increased insomnia, fatigue, muscle aches, and other strange symptoms that are resulting from this. Some are also reporting feeling increased activity in their third eye, seeing visions and drawing on energetic information from the Universe. How you may be experiencing these symptoms ultimately depends on you. You may experience many, or none at all. This does not mean anything is wrong with you. Of course, any time you experience alarming symptoms with your physical or mental health you should always consult a healthcare professional. However, if it comes up that nothing is wrong, recognize that there is a good chance that it is just you experiencing the energetic ascension of Earth itself.

During the ascension process of Earth energies, it is important to take extra time nourishing your energies and taking care of yourself. As an Empath, you will be experiencing these energies more than anyone else. This means that you need to take extra precautions, while also ramping up your efforts to connect with yourself and lead by example. This is a great time to be awakening if you are presently in the process, even though you may be feeling many symptoms that make it feel otherwise. Know that these symptoms will not last forever. Your gift, however, will.

Final Words

Congratulations on completing *"Highly Sensitive Empaths: The Complete Survival Guide to Self-Discovery, Protection from Narcissists and Energy Vampires, and Developing the Empath Gift."*

Being an Empath is a great treasure that is only bestowed on those who can handle it. Since you were born an Empath, you can guarantee that this is a gift that you can manage well. Even if it has not felt that way yet, trust that it is only because there have not been enough resources available for you to support you in mastering this gift.

I hope this book becomes a great resource for you in supporting you in understanding yourself more. I also hope that you are now able to take advantage of better self-care tools to protect you and keep you feeling like you are giving from a full cup. If you have been dealing with abusive people in your life, I hope that you do take the time to understand that this is not because there is anything inherently wrong with you. Narcissistic people are drawn to you to as you have the one thing they do not: empathy. As a bonus, you've got a whole lot of it, too.

The next step for you is to take some time learning what self-care measures work best for you. While being an Empath is similar for everyone, you are still human and will still have different needs from others in your life. Creating a self-care method that supports your needs and allows you to feel truly nourished and cared for is important. Take your time working through different strategies until you find the routine that fits for you. Then, make sure that you always set aside time to fulfill that routine and keep yourself taken care of. It is essential that you always put yourself first, even though you may feel that this is "wrong" because of the way you are wired. Trust that if you want to help others, helping yourself first is the best way to do so. It is also important to realize that in many cases, the best way you can help is by becoming a role model. It is never helpful to anyone for you to take on the responsibility of others.

As well, be sure to take advantage of the many online communities that are built around being an Empath. With having access to the internet, taking advantage of these communities gives you the opportunity to meet and connect with other individuals who have similar experiences as you. This will ensure that you are able to access support and understanding from other Empaths. As an Empath, not having other Empaths in your life who speak the same language as you can be challenging. It may even lead you to feeling isolated. Having access to those who will understand and show the same degree of Empathy and compassion that you do when you are experiencing things in your life can be extremely helpful.

Being an Empath can be challenging if you do not have access to the right resources, but once you do, you begin to see the blessing and beauty in the gift that you have been given. Be sure to give yourself the opportunity to fully flourish in your gift so you can live your best life.

Lastly, if you enjoyed the book *"Highly Sensitive Empaths: The Complete Survival Guide to Self-Discovery, Protection from Narcissists and Energy Vampires, and Developing the Empath Gift"* please take the time to leave a kind review on Amazon. Your honest feedback would be greatly appreciated.

Thank you, and best of luck in your journey.

If you forgot to sign up to the newsletter and receive you free eBook on "6 Ways to Thrive as an Empath and Live a great Life" here is the link below.

<u>http://bit.ly/6WaysToThriveAsAnEmpath</u>

Emotional and Narcissistic Abuse

The Complete Survival Guide to
Understanding Narcissism, Escaping the
Narcissist in a Toxic Relationship Forever,
and Your Road to Recovery

J. Vandeweghe

Free E-book and Newsletter

PERSEVERING THROUGH 'NO-CONTACT' HANDBOOK

Click the link below to sign up to the newsletter and receive a free Handbook on Persevering Through 'No-Contact.' There is some helpful advice in there and a great source to turn to when you in moments of struggle.

http://bit.ly/No-Contact-Handbook

Introduction

Thank you for purchasing *"Emotional and Narcissistic Abuse: The Complete Survival Guide to Understanding Narcissism, Escaping the Narcissist in a Toxic Relationship Forever, and Your Road to Recovery."*

If you are reading this book, it is likely because you are seeking support for leaving from an abusive, narcissistic relationship. Or want to find ways to heal. This book has been written to inform you on narcissism, narcissistic personality disorder, the cycles of abuse, the symptoms of the relationship, the damage to the victim, and how you can safely escape and heal from a narcissistic relationship.

While this book goes into depth on all of the information you need to know regarding narcissism and the abusive relationships you may endure with a narcissistic partner, it is important to understand that this book does not substitute a professional therapist. Abusive relationships can be tricky and, as you will learn, the depth of the trauma can be deep in these types of relationships. Having access to a professionally trained therapist can be vital in helping you heal from everything you go through, including understanding what happened and healing from it all.

That being said, this book will provide you with great value and insight on everything you are going through and what you need to do next. If you are still in the relationship, this will support you in the process of beginning to demystify everything that has been going on and recognizing the reality of what you are experiencing. As you will learn, this is an essential part of breaking free from the relationship and healing.

I hope that this book finds you well and safe and that everything within these pages supports you in understanding more about your relationship. I also hope it helps you to safely leave your relationship so that you can move on to the healing process and eventually resume a happy, healthy lifestyle. Remember, it is never your fault.

Chapter 1: A Narcissistic Love Story

This is the story of a narcissist and his (or her) victim. This is the story that every narcissistic abuse victim will recognize and understand. It is a painful truth of the life of someone who is in love with a narcissist. For the purpose of this story, the narcissist has been referred to as a male. It should be noted that NOT all narcissists are male.

"You recall the beginning when it was so sweet and so pure. It began simply: with love and tenderness. The chemistry was insanely powerful, so much so that you felt like you had known this person for life. It was effortless. Whenever you were with him, you felt higher and higher. It was a match made in heaven, or so you thought.

Every conversation you shared, every text you sent, felt so right. He made you feel like the only person in the world – like you were his one true love. Like this would have a fairytale ending. This was going to be your happy ending, and you were ready for your Prince Charming to whisk you away on his white horse. Until you realized Prince Charming was not so charming and his horse was nowhere to be found.

It was not too long before you began to see the mask slip. The face he carefully curated just for his entertainment, to reel you in, began to fall off. It started slowly, a single incident amidst the perfect relationship. Everything else was so right that you managed to justify these behaviors. After all, he helped you do it, didn't he? He told you it was work, or you did something to upset him. He was entirely justified in his actions. He was still your perfect Prince Charming.

Everything went back to normal until it happened again. This time his rage grew stronger, more powerful. He carefully crafted together a fabric of falsehoods. He used the worst miseries from your past and the most intense insecurities from your present to justify his behavior. It's your fault for upsetting him, or not trusting him. You should have known better. What were you thinking?

Slowly, he introduces new ways to torment you. More people enter the scene, consistently tearing away from your Prince Charming relationship. He praises them and shames you. Winning is his favorite pass-time, and when he sees you squirm, he knows he is winning this game.

Your reality begins to turn into a falsehood that he creates for you. You grow more and more doubtful of your inner voice, allowing you to justify his behavior further. You knew he didn't like that, why did you do it anyway? His actions are your fault. You did this. Every strength you have becomes a flaw, every talent you have is a travesty, and all of your compassion is just you being naïve. He takes over your reality, stripping away your identity, memory, and self-esteem. Rapidly, his weaknesses are your weaknesses, and he projects every inch of his reality unto you. Your mind drips his stories, and you hungrily eat them up. Your reality is no longer your own. It is his now. He has taken over.

The narcissist does not believe in true love until the love becomes addicting. Until it becomes a game of give-and-take. One where he gives the abuse and takes your self-confidence, self-worth, and identity away completely. One where he gives you poison and takes away the real antidote.

You begin to question yourself and everything he has done. You can feel the cruelty, but you start to wonder if it was really meant to be cruel or not. Maybe it was a mistake? Perhaps he did not realize what he was doing? Your once carefree, lighthearted and loving spirit fades as you begin to feel insecure and oversensitive. You wonder if you are crazy. You question everything your insides tell you. Is this real? Is any of this real?

As you crumble and find yourself struggling to decipher reality from this falsehood, he continues to hide his intentions and layer on the abuse. He showers you with gentle love and sprinkles you with condescending contempt. You can never decide what is what. You are continually being poisoned and then remedied, over and over and over again.

Each time the love is taken away, and you are left in the midst of the cruelty, you find yourself reeling. Withdrawal from this drug is painful, and you so desperately need your next fix. Your addiction validates his destruction. This is how he knows he is winning the game. He has you right where he wants you.

The abuse accelerates to the point that you are now admitting defeat toward it all on a daily basis. He becomes meaner and meaner, testing you to see how far he can take it. Will you take it? He accelerates from harsh words and sarcastic jabs to condescending put-downs and full-out attacks. The entire relationship is a power play, and he refuses to let you win this battle for dominance. Instead, he makes you feel like you are winning from time to time, only so he can strike you down once more.

Each time you default to defeat faster, he rips you apart further. The wounds layer upon you, cutting away at who you are and locking you within his mental prison. He abuses you while forcing you to doubt the abuse, leading you to believe there is no abuse genuinely happening in this relationship. Your quiet inner voice screams out for protection, but the voice he has grown within you silences it and pushes you to believe him and hold on to the false reality of who this man really is.

The fairy tale has ended, but you no longer have the strength or ability to walk away. You are left facing the nightmare. This is no longer a game that he (or she) needs to win. This is a nightmare that you need to awaken from. Perhaps you will awaken from it over and over, awaiting the opportunity for you to realize that you are no longer dreaming and this is all very real.

In this love story, the happy ending is not one of romance and forever-after. This happy ending lies in you realizing Prince Charming never existed, and this was all a twisted game of narcissist-and-mouse."

Chapter 2: The Real Narcissist

The casual tossing-around of the word "narcissist" has led many people to falsely believe that a narcissist is simply someone who has an inflated sense of confidence and perhaps a slightly inflated ego, too. Unfortunately, the dictionary reinforces this belief with its description of a narcissist, stating that they are "a person who has an excessive interest in or admiration of themselves." This is more likely to be the definition of someone who is arrogant and not someone who is narcissistic. The reality of a narcissist is much darker than that.

Narcissists do tend to think incredibly highly of themselves, but the reality of who they are and what they do is extremely intricate and well-played. Narcissism is an intricate, well-constructed series of traits wrapped up in one mental illness that is extremely damaging to all who cross the paths of a narcissist, especially their lovers.

Some people are known to possess narcissistic-like qualities, but this is entirely different from what a true narcissist is. A true narcissist is a master at lying, phenomenal at deception, and incredibly talented at curating codependent victims. They are powerful. Because a narcissist is generally slow and consistent in their approach, they are masters at tearing down other people to the point that the other person develops an addiction to the narcissist. The narcissist is not just in love with getting attention; they are completely addicted to it. That is the basis for their entire mental illness. It is what drives them and what results in them masterfully playing out all of their puppeteering behaviors.

Who is a Narcissist?
If you ask someone who a narcissist is, most people will describe an arrogant, entitled, privileged male. This is the persona that has been promoted as "narcissist" in most people's lives. However, the reality is that narcissists are not quite as defined as that. A narcissist can truly be anyone. There is no preferred gender, age, or race that narcissism chooses. Instead, anyone can be a narcissist.

In the United States, it is estimated that 1 in every 25 people is a sociopath. As you will learn about later in this chapter, sociopaths are those who are at the top end of the spectrum that also contains psychopaths and narcissists. The number of narcissistic individuals living in modern America is surprisingly large. The majority of us come across at least one in our lives that impacts us in some way. For some of us, that impact is significant. For others, they recognize the behavior to be negative and walk away.

Rather than looking at the demographics of "who" a narcissist is, it is easier to identify one by their traits. The list of characteristics that a narcissist has that identifies their narcissistic behaviors is reasonably straightforward and is the easiest way to determine a narcissist. Attempting to use statistical evidence around their demographic will not result in an accurate finding.

What are the Traits of a Narcissist?

Paying attention to the traits of an individual is the easiest way to identify whether or not someone is a narcissist. If you want to identify one, pay attention to the list of traits below and take a moment to consider if the person you are questioning possesses these traits. This will support you in understanding if they truly are a narcissist.

People with narcissistic personality disorder possess these traits:

A Complete Lack of Empathy

First and foremost, someone who is narcissistic possesses a complete lack of empathy. Those with a narcissistic personality disorder do not simply lack empathy; they are mentally incapable of experiencing it. This results in them being incapable of identifying the emotions or feelings of others and taking them into account.

Due to a lack of empathy, people who are narcissistic will struggle to behave in a way that shows any compassion toward other humans. They are incapable of understanding how their actions impact others, and as a result, they are known to regularly behave in a way that is mentally damaging to others. This is how they build on their abuse without showing any signs of feeling remorseful for it: because they truly cannot feel remorse. It can be very toxic and draining to be around someone who has so sign of empathy nor takes responsibility for their actions.

Grandiose Sense of Self-Importance

People who are narcissistic are known to have an elated sense of self-importance. They will often lie about their achievements to make them sound better than they are. They also lie about their talents so that people will believe they are more capable than they actually are. A narcissist does not just want to be recognized and superior and better, they expect to be. Regardless of what their actual achievements are, even if they are incredibly few or irrelevant, they expect to be seen as the superior person. No matter what, a narcissist wants to be seen as better than everyone else they meet.

Fantasizes About Unlimited Power or Success

Narcissistic people are obsessed with their fantasies about unlimited power and success. They like to fantasize about being better than everyone else in every way possible, from their looks to their life. They want to be the best at activities, in relationships, in their family, at work, and in virtually every area of their life. They will do everything they can to make it appear as though they have the best life possible and that it is better than anyone else's. This enables narcissists to have an unrealistic belief of what their life truly is, which often provides a strong basis for how they are able to deceive other people into believing their fantasy reality versus the actual reality.

Believe They are "Special"

Individuals who are narcissistic have a belief that they are "special" in some way. This promotes their inner belief that they are superior to others and why they act so entitled. They believe that they are only capable of being understood by other "special" people, who are typically only those of high-status. In fact, many believe they should only associate with people of high-status or institutions of high-status and often think that they are above everyone else. This belief can be seen in their arrogant behaviors, their attitude toward other people, and the way that they talk themselves up in groups.

Addicted to Attention

The narcissist's addiction to attention is the driving force behind everything that they do. Narcissists do not just crave attention; they *need* it. This is why they will lie about everything, fantasize about massive success and power, and otherwise focus on things that will earn them some attention including drama. They may be particularly focused on grooming and maintaining a very poised outward image (their mask, or false-self: see Chapter 5). This is how they are able to draw in all of the attention they crave from other people.

Because of their need for attention, narcissists become abusive. Their carefully crafted abuse cycle enables them to cause other people to become codependent, resulting in these other people not having a sense of self-worth or identity. Then, they are pressured to see this individual as the "godly" aspect of their lives. The codependent will look to the narcissist for validation, approval, and acceptance. The narcissist will offer increments of validation, approval, and acceptances in dosages that become increasingly smaller over time. At first, their withholding of love and kindness only happens every once in a while. Eventually, it happens daily.

Is Envious or Believes Others Are Envious

Narcissists tend to go one or both ways with envy. They either tend to be chronically envious of everyone else which further drives their need for attention, or they believe that everyone else is envious of them. Most narcissists are both to a degree.

When they are envious of others, the narcissist will rarely say anything. Instead, they will begin to lie and exploit others, even more, to make it appear as though they are not envious and have nothing to be envious about. Remember, a narcissist does not only want to be the best in the room, but they truly believe they *are* at all times. They will say anything they need to say to ensure that everyone else believes this mask and regards them as the best, even if that includes lying, manipulating people, exploiting others, and otherwise being abusive to the people they know and, in many cases, do not know.

When they believe others are envious of them, this feeds into their need for attention. They feel good – like they are winning at their game. They want other people to be envious of them because this is how people feel toward people who are "better." At least, that is what the narcissist believes. The narcissist will say and do anything it takes to ensure they are better than the others, even if they really are not, just so that the other people in the room become envious of them. This supports their need for attention and thus becomes one of their favorite tools for satisfying the addiction.

Arrogant Behavior or Attitude
Despite arrogance itself not being the measure of a narcissist, most narcissists are arrogant. This means that not all arrogant people are narcissists, but all narcissists are arrogant. This arrogant behavior and attitude supports them in promoting themselves as the best person in the room. It allows them to portray a higher degree of confidence then they actually possess, allowing them to appear "special" and better than others.

When a narcissist is arrogant, they are the maximum degree of arrogant they can possibly be. They are not just slightly arrogant or walking around with a somewhat inflated ego and sense of self-confidence. People with narcissistic personality disorder take arrogance to the next level. They are extremely inflated in their confidence and ego about absolutely everything. This is a tool they use to appear better, and they use it to the maximum degree.

Compulsive Liars
Narcissists are compulsive liars. As such, they are also experts at manipulating other people. Narcissists will expertly create a web of lies that support them in creating their desired reality and bringing other people into it. If they are ever caught in a lie, they will masterfully create more lies to cover up the lies that they have already told. In this process, they are not worried about who they hurt or who they blame through their lies. Their only concern is in ensuring that they are protected and that they come out looking like the winner in one way or another.

When a narcissist is not outright lying, they will purposefully leave out important pieces of information. Or, they will stonewall the victim by refusing to answer any questions or by providing evasive answers to the questions being asked. This is another way of them creating a blameless crime where they can easily spin it around to look like it was someone else's fault for not asking for the information outright, even though they knew that the chances of the other person thinking to ask would be slim. This is how they ensure that even when they are lying, they cannot be blamed for their lies. If anything, you can be blamed for not pressing for more information.

No matter how much you continue digging to discover what the full truth is or attempting to untangle their lies, you will never get to the real truth. They will continue dancing around the situation until you are so exhausted that you stop. If you do not exhaust before finally reaching their breaking point, you will be so tired from chasing that you are no longer able to fight or stand up for yourself, thus meaning you are still a victim of the lie even if you finally get to the truth. Either way, the narcissist wins.

Openly Exploits Victims on Social Media
A narcissist has a deep addiction to exploiting their victims. These days, social media has given them the power to exploit, even more, resulting in their victims suffering even further. There are at least five major ways that narcissists will take advantage of social media to exploit you, should they so desire.

The first way is by using social media to enhance further their favorite abuse tool of "triangulation," which you will learn about in greater depth in Chapter 7. In essence, they will bring another person into the mixture and embarrass you by giving more attention to the other person then is typically reasonable or acceptable for a relationship. This may lead to you believing they are cheating because they share pictures of them with this other person, or they comment more on their photos than they do on yours, thus making it clearly visible that this other person is getting more attention than you do. Then, when you attempt to point this act out, they will blame you for overreacting or reading something into it when they claim that nothing is actually happening.

They will also use social media as a way to spy on you. Narcissists will often follow you on social media and pay attention to your goings on online to see what you are doing and see anything that they could use against you. This helps them learn more about what you like, what you are interested in, how you speak to your friends, and otherwise. Later, they will use this information in their love-bombing stage where they attract your attention and get you to fall in love with them. Then, they will use this exact same information to abuse you by calling you names or ridiculing you for your various interests and the things you post or share.

Not only will a narcissist spy on you during the relationship and use the information against you, but they will also use it after the relationship ends as a way to stalk and harass you. If you have ever tried to leave the relationship in the past, you can likely recall them stalking everything you are doing and regularly messaging you and trying to get in touch with you so that they could attempt to lure you back into the relationship. This is done in a way that is enough to feel like a clear violation but is typically not done so much so that it violates harassment laws enough to result in any type of persecution.

They will also use social media as a way to embellish their grandiose sense of self. They will post only images that they feel boosts their popularity and social status as a way to feed their constant need for attention. Then, when they actually get likes, they will use this as a way to make others look lesser to them because they are not getting as much attention. Therefore, they can make it look like the other person is not cared about or likable. If you are in a relationship with these people, they will likely use you as a way to increase their popularity. For example, they may post provocative pictures of you or ones that make you look bad in some way but can be twisted to make them look good. This makes you look like the lesser person in the relationship and, as a result of their manipulation, makes them look like the good person even though they are posting pictures without your consent that show you off in a bad, uncomfortable, or inappropriate way. Not only does this feed their need to look good, but it can also further isolate you from others in your life because it may cause those you are close with to begin thinking less of you and believing that you are engaging in negative behavior, rather than the true fact which is that the person you were with exploited you and treated you abusively.

Lastly, social media provides an excellent platform for narcissists to bully and taunt other people. Online, narcissists take pleasure in provoking people to begin engaging in an argument but spin the entire thing to make it look like it is the other persons' fault. They tend to be extremely cruel and violent, often threatening peoples' physical wellbeing or livelihood altogether.

Talks Behind People's Backs
Social media is not the only place where a narcissist will exploit their victims. Narcissists also like to talk behind people's backs when they are not around as a way to make them look better and create drama. One of the most frustrating things about this is that it can take an awfully long time before you realize this is happening. The narcissist is incredibly smart and tactical when it comes to these games. When you do realize, it becomes very painful and challenging to accept, especially when these accusations remarks about you are completely false. In virtually every scenario where you are not around, and the narcissist sees an opportunity to use you to increase their sense of self, and harm your social image, they will. Typically, this talk will be degrading and will result in you being made out to sound like you are worthless, incapable and despised while the narcissist appears to always come out as the hero in the story. To them, it is a way of making themselves look great. For you, it can feel like they are making you out to sound like some form of an incompetent fool.

Energy Vampires
Because of their compulsive lying, the constant need for attention, addiction to drama and their grandiose sense of self, narcissists are one of the highest forms of the energy vampire. They require a lot of time and attention from other people, often resulting in them willing to go to extreme lengths to get it. If you are in a relationship with them, they will naturally rely on you to be their main source of energy. When things become stagnant, the narcissist loves to create completely false accusations and situations to put you on the back foot and defend

yourself. The narcissist loves creating drama and fights as a way to suck the energy out of you and make you work harder for their love and approval. As such, you may find yourself feeling constantly drained and exhausted by them. They will leach onto your energy until they can no longer do so because you are exhausted and have no energy left to give. Once they see you reach this weakened state, they will initiate the part of their abuse cycle where they begin to decimate your sense of self-esteem and self-confidence. This will drive you to a breaking point where you can no longer handle their abuse. Then, when you are just about ready to give up and find your freedom or peace, they come back with their love-bombing and try to refuel your energy tank. This result's in a deep battle between you and them where you long to get away and feel free once again, but their energy vampire traits result's in a vicious roller-coaster ride.

High Sex Drive

Energy is transferred in large amounts through sexual acts. For this reason, many narcissists have an incredibly high sex drive. They always want to have sex with you, exploit you during sex, and be made to feel like they are the "dominant" one during their sex with you. This is because they get a lot of energy out of this experience. It also is a great way for them to amplify the roller-coaster-like abuse-cycle. If they have been super-abusive to you lately and feel you slipping away from their web, they may try to love-bomb you with attention and sex. Because they are having sex with you, they will often make it seem like it will be a mutually enjoyable experience. That is until it begins. Once you start having sex with them, most of the time they generally become selfish lovers and will only engage in the forms of sex that they want. If they do happen to give in to what you want, you can almost always guarantee that it will come back on you later as a situation where "I let you ____, so you owe me!" or "I did ____ which is proof of how much I love you!" type statements are used. This is a way to twist it to seem like they are generous and considerate of your feelings, but later they use this generosity as a way to get their own needs met and send yours down once again.

Inability to Feel Guilt or Remorse

As a result of their lack of empathy, narcissists have a complete inability to feel guilty or remorseful for anything that they have done. They are literally incapable, meaning that no matter what you do or say they will never truly feel bad for their actions. However, this is not always apparent at first glance. In many instances, when it serves them, narcissists will *mimic* guilt or remorse as a way to make it appear as though they are genuinely sorry for what they have done or that they genuinely feel bad for creating chaos or destruction in your life in one way or another. This, however, is absolutely never a real sense of guilt or remorse. Instead, it is their way of getting you to believe that they did not have any ill intentions, thus allowing them to jump back on track to serve their own needs quickly. In some cases, they realize that arguing with you over their mistakes may take away too much from their end goal: to win. So, they will use their fake remorse as a way to avoid the hassle and get to where they want to be even faster. Plus, they can use this as "evidence" that they do feel bad when they hurt you, thus giving them the opportunity to make you sound crazy for believing that they always hurt you intentionally and without any concern. This keeps you roped in and believing their lies for as long as possible. Eventually, there will come a time where it is clearly evident that they are incapable of feeling remorseful or guilty for their actions. It is a painful truth to face and can be extremely difficult to comprehend how someone can be so cruel and numb. By this time, it is usually too late and you are deeply in the abuse cycle.

Inability to Apologize or Admit Wrong-doing
One thing that you can guarantee about a narcissist is that they will never admit to being wrong. Narcissists do not, under any circumstances, apologize for their behavior or actions. They absolutely never will. If they do, you must never believe that this is a true admission of their mistake. Instead, they are using it as a bargaining chip to twist it around and make it sound like they made a mistake either because they were forced to (which transfers the blame away from them) or because it was supportive of the bigger picture (which in the end only feeds their needs and ego). The other time they will apologize is when you have done absolutely everything in your power to get them to apologize, and they have effectively sucked the life out of you, so they throw you a bone. But you can be absolutely sure there

110

will be no truth or meaning to their apology. There is virtually never a sincere admission of a mistake from a narcissist. Why would they apologize to you when they don't even feel any sense of guilt or remorse for what they have done? Instead, they are more likely to lie and create another false sense of reality. Be aware of this.

Experts at Playing the Victim

Another trait narcissists carry as a result of being masters at manipulating is their ability to "turn the tables" and project onto others. Narcissists love to twist the switch around so that it seems like *you* were actually the one to do something that *they* did. For example, say you are in the middle of an argument, and a narcissist begins calling you names and bullying you. If you were to later in the argument point this out and call them out on it, the narcissist would start projecting, saying that you were the one bullying them and anything they said was only a means of defending themselves against your bullying. This means that they can expertly become the victim of any situation and make you out to be the attacker. Because you are not the one playing the head games, but instead you are the real victim, what can end up happening is two situations.

1. You feel the guilt and remorse that they are incapable of feeling. You will likely begin questioning your own actions and looking to verify what they have said. If they point out any specific evidence, you will immediately start feeling bad and trying to make up for what you have said or done, even though you likely never announced or did it with any malicious intent. As a result, they end up with the upper hand, and you are left apologizing to them and trying to make up for what you supposedly did when in reality they are the ones behaving in an abusive manner. Or:
2. You are familiar with these games the narcissist plays, and often these false accusations and acts of victimization can lead to extreme cases of confusion and frustration. You can't even comprehend how the "tables are being turned" onto you now. Ultimately, your acts of confusion and frustration which can lead to more arguing and fighting are going to fuel the narcissist even more and significantly drain the energy out of you. Either way, the narcissist wins in this situation.

I hope this list of traits has been eye-opening for you and you have been able to confidently identify a narcissist you may have in your life after reading this list of characteristics. Awareness is the first step. Once you know what you're dealing with, you can begin making the correct choices towards your recovery.

What is the Narcissistic Spectrum?

The narcissistic spectrum is a spectrum of personality disorders that feature zero empathy. These individuals range from narcissistic tendencies to narcissistic personality disorders. At the top end of the spectrum, you will also find sociopathy and psychopathy. These personality disorders all range in the same spectrum because each of them lacks empathy in varying degrees, ranging from difficulties with experiencing empathy to a complete inability to experience empathy. *Some* people on the spectrum can mimic empathy and use this to allow them to blend into society better. These individuals tend to be on the lower end of the spectrum. Others completely lack empathy and are incapable of recognizing it in any degree. They cannot fake empathy. These are sociopaths, and they are generally hazardous people since they can behave in ruthless and violent ways and experience no emotional repercussions from it.

When someone is narcissistic, they may be on the spectrum with narcissistic tendencies, or they may have a full-blown narcissistic personality disorder. Narcissistic tendencies mean that they experience some or most of the traits expressed in the previous section. A full-blown narcissistic personality disorder is seen in individuals who have absolutely no empathy and who suffer every single attribute of the personality disorder, often to a fairly extreme degree.

Chapter 3: The Silent Abuser

Narcissism is known as the "silent abuser" because it tends to creep up on you and you do not notice it until it feels too late to get out. By the time you recognize the abuse, your reality has been distorted, and you have been completely stripped of self-confidence, self-worth, and identity. This results in it being extremely challenging to remove yourself from these situations.

Let's explore what narcissistic abuse is really like and how it actually impacts the victim, particularly in romantic relationships.

A Frog in Boiling Water

The best way to describe narcissistic abuse and why victims tend to remain stuck in the situation is by the "frog in boiling water" analogy. The theory is as follows: if you were to put a frog in boiling water, it would immediately jump out because it knew it was dangerous and it could die. Likewise, if you were to enter a relationship that was obviously abusive from the beginning, you would have left it because you could easily recognize the signs of abuse from the start.

However, if you put a frog in a pot of room-temperature water and slowly increase the temperature over time until it is boiling, the frog will stay in the pot of water until it cooks and dies. This is because the frog never knew when to jump out. It seemed manageable until suddenly it was too hot and the frog could no longer physically get out. Likewise, when you enter a relationship with a narcissist, it is usually incredible in the beginning. There are typically zero signs of abuse. The abuser builds up a persona for you that results in them appearing to be your "one true love." They will do everything to earn your love and make you feel like everything is perfect and you have finally found someone who gets you and who you can settle down with. Then, the abuse slowly starts creeping in. At first, it only happens once in a while. This is how the narcissist can start distorting your reality. They encourage you both to shrug it off as "just a one-time thing." As you begin to agree and shrug it off, they begin to do it more and more. As it increases, your tolerance for their abuse grows. That is until it is eventually so much that you cannot handle it. Before you know it, the abuse is happening daily, and you are justifying it because you have been conditioned to. Because your reality has been distorted, you begin to question yourself. You have been conditioned to accept the abuse and brush it off. Now, like the frog, you are trapped in the boiling water, and it feels almost impossible to leave.

For anyone who is the victim of a narcissistic relationship, this tends to be one of the most challenging parts to accept. Realizing that everything from the earliest moments of your relationship together has been a lie is a tough reality to accept, especially when you are in love. The constant battle between reality and fantasy makes it very hard to leave. Many people are not ready to recognize or admit that this behavior is going on, instead wanting to fight for what they have together because they are afraid of losing the "good" aspects of the relationship. To the narcissist, however, this is all a game. They derive great joy from "hooking" new victims into their abuse cycle, as to them this is part of the joy of a new relationship. For you, it was the intense bursts of love and joy that created the excitement. For the narcissist, it was the sly win that resulted in them coming home with a brand-new prize to abuse and use to fulfill their own selfish needs: you. The narcissist knows that they are creating power over you as time goes on and the more you tolerate their behavior, the more they realize their win is guaranteed. They always start slowly, ensuring that you are not fully aware of what is going on. As your tolerance increases, so do the instances of abuse and wrongdoings. While you are falling in love with them, in spite of their "flaws," they are falling in love with how you are serving them and their dangerous and unhealthy needs.

Signs of Narcissistic Abuse

If you have been abused by a narcissist, you will have symptoms that prove the abuse. These symptoms are challenging. They result in severe psychological trauma to those who have been abused by the narcissist. The signs of narcissistic abuse arise only after the initial love-bombing stops and the narcissist begins their cycle of destroying you. Because it is early on and you are still full of energy and positivity, this part is particularly enjoyable to the narcissist. It also tends to go undetected to you because it starts out slow. They gradually chip away at every positive trait you have, either decimating it or twisting it to be seen as something small, embarrassing, or otherwise unnecessary and pointless. As they scoop these traits out of you, they emphasize all of your bad qualities and press your negativity up, really making it appear like you have nothing positive to give. You only really begin to notice the signs and become aware of this *after* all of your positive traits have been scooped out, and you are left feeling like the worst possible version of yourself. Once you have reached this point, you begin to recognize all of the symptoms of your abuse. At this point, however, it generally feels too late because so much damage has already been done. If you are beginning to reach this point yourself, you may notice the following signs and symptoms arising in your own life.

Using Dissociation as a Survival Mechanism

Individuals who have been abused by a narcissist begin to practice dissociation to protect themselves. Dissociation allows them to detach from their environment, which can disrupt your memory, perceptions, consciousness, and sense of self.

When you experience dissociation, it allows you to numb yourself to the trauma you are facing. You may find yourself using mind-numbing activities, addictions, or obsessions as a strategy to support you in repressing your reality. Often, victims will find themselves slowly becoming more and more addicted to things like video games, scrolling social media, skimming books, cooking, or even taking medications as a way to keep their mind numb to what is happening. Some might even begin experiencing obsessive behavior, finding themselves obsessing over how to maintain their environment "just so" to minimize the abuse and to protect themselves against the dangers of the narcissist. This is how you are able to block out the impact emotionally, so you do not have to feel the pain and the entirety of your circumstances.

This dissociation may also result in you having various parts of your personality that are only experienced and expressed at certain times. You may completely change around certain people or in specific circumstances so that you can support these fragmented versions of who you are. Integrating and reclaiming these disowned pieces of your personality is necessary for you to create a cohesive narrative. This is how you are able to then incorporate your emotional, cognitive and physiological realities together. The best way to seek help on this specific symptom is to receive support from a therapist who is trauma-informed.

Questioning What is Real
One of the primary goals of a narcissist is to suck you into their false reality and isolate you from true reality. This can result in you living a life where the true reality that everyone else is living feels questionable to you. You become confused. Over time, you are conditioned to see the reality the narcissist projects onto you. This reality is one that is self-serving on behalf of the narcissist, causing you to live, breathe, eat, and sleep to their benefit. In this reality that you are sucked into, you are nothing more than a servant of the narcissist's reality. The idea of doing things in a world where everything does not revolve around this person can seem daunting and unlikely. This is because the narcissist has expertly roped you into their world and caused you to divorce your own.

One major symptom that results in you having a dissociation from true reality is memory problems. Many victims of narcissists doubt their own memory and their own view of reality, often relying on the narcissist to feed them what their reality is. This happens because, over the course of the relationship, your very real recollection of events is distorted and twisted by the manipulative narcissist. This can lead to you doubting your own judgment and believing in only what the narcissist says. This happens both as a result of manipulation, sheer energetic exhaustion and a growing inability to fight back. What ends up happening is your own recollection of events and understanding of the world no longer feels valid to you because it has been invalidated and twisted by the narcissist for so long, it can be easy to no longer trust your own perception. The battle of searching between truth and fantasy can be incredibly daunting and exhausting. Becoming so confused and wrapped up in the narcissist's web of lies is traumatizing. You become so confused you don't know what to believe which can make it very difficult to escape the narcissist.

Feeling Like You are Constantly Walking on Egg Shells

Individuals who are being subjected to abuse often feel like they are always walking on eggshells. This is common of people who have experienced trauma in their relationship. It may feel as though you are still afraid of creating a problem, and so you are cautious about what you say and what you do. When it comes to narcissism, in particular, it can be challenging to identify precisely what will set the other person off in some cases. For that reason, your space may feel even more volatile. Certain things may set the narcissist off sometimes but not at other times. This can create even more confusion and frustration within you. You may feel perpetual anxiety looming within you that at any moment you could "provoke" your abuser. This often leads to a fear of confrontation and a lack of boundaries because you do not want to upset the other person.

Sacrificing Yourself to Please the Abuser

If you are the victim of a narcissist, there is a good chance that you regularly find yourself sacrificing your needs, desires, and maybe even your safety to please your abuser. You might recall a time where you had goals, hopes, and dreams and now you no longer work toward these. You might feel like you are alive only to fulfill the needs and agenda of another person and that you are not allowed to or able to satisfy your own needs and desires. At first, it may have seemed like the narcissist's entire world revolved around you. However, over time it will have flipped, and now your whole world might revolve around them.

Everything from your goals, friendships, hobbies, and even personal safety have probably taken a back seat to your need to keep your abuser feeling "satisfied" within your relationship. Though, you will soon begin to realize that there is no way for you to actually ever satisfy your abuser because they are insatiable.

Health Issues and Somatic Symptoms of Your Abuse
Individuals who are being abused, especially by a narcissist, are known to have common health issues and somatic symptoms that are directly related to the abuse. This can include excessive weight gain or weight loss, serious health issues that did not exist prior to the relationship, or physical symptoms that show premature aging. Because of the constant abuse, your body has been under chronic stress and has been producing massive amounts of cortisol. As a result, you begin to have many health challenges.

These health challenges do not simply remain in the physical, either. You may find yourself experiencing anxiety and depression, or even considering self-harm or suicidal ideation. In fact, many people who are subjected to abuse will begin to practice self-harm as a result of the deterioration of their mental health. Another common experience from those being abused is a difficulty sleeping. You may find it challenging to sleep and, when you do, you may find that you have nightmares that wake you. These nightmares are ultimately you reliving the trauma through emotional or visual flashbacks that continually bring you back to the abuse.

The more you remain in the relationship with the narcissist, the worse these stress-related symptoms will become. Because the narcissist is continuously feeding on your energy and emotions to fulfill their own needs, you have nothing left for yourself. Any time you feel any level of positive energy within you, the narcissist will see this energy and take it for themselves, leaving you frustrated and without energy once again. They will continuously push you, striving to get an emotional reaction out of you in any way they can. Through these constant and intense emotional reactions that you are forced into, you grow even more stressed out and wary. Soon, your mental, physical, and emotional well-being are severely compromised, making it even harder for you to fight your way to safety. The stress becomes so high that many victims of the abuse begin to contemplate suicide and other drastic measures of escaping because they are no longer hopeful of a happy life.

You Cannot Trust Other People
Due to the mental abuse you face from the narcissist, you may find that you can no longer trust anyone. Everyone who enters your life may now represent a threat to you in your life. You may become anxious, doubting the intentions of others and assuming for the worst to happen in all scenarios. This becomes even worse because you have experienced the malicious actions of someone who you once trusted but who ended up becoming an abuser toward you. A standard caution turns into hyper-vigilance as you become incredibly aware of anyone and everyone who enters your surroundings and your life.

Because the narcissistic abuser has worked so hard to gaslight you, you no longer believe your experiences are valid. Thus it is a challenge for you to trust anyone including yourself. Even if you feel inside that someone is safe or trustworthy, you may feel as though they are going to hurt you or struggle to actually trust them because of what you experienced in the past.

Self-Isolating Behaviors
The majority of abusers will use isolation as a way to keep their victims away from receiving any help. However, many victims of abuse are also known to isolate themselves. This happens out of shame. Due to the amount of victim-blaming and misconceptions about emotional and psychological violence in society, many victims struggle to trust anyone to support them. In fact, some may be further traumatized by law enforcement, family members, friends, and the friends of the narcissist who may all work toward invalidating the victim's experiences and also promoting the narcissist's behavior. Another common reason why victims will isolate themselves is that they no longer have the energy to

deal with anyone else. After having all of their energy sucked up by the narcissist, they do not have what it takes to leave the house, engage with friends or family, or even make a basic phone call to chat with anyone they care about. What small energy the victim has remaining is needed to keep themselves alive and do the very basic self-care acts. Otherwise, they often spend their time quietly tucked away on their own attempting to regain the energy that was stolen from them.

Because the victim lives in fear, believing that no one will understand them, they also fail to reach out for help. Instead, they isolate themselves to protect themselves from further abuse. This is how they relieve themselves of judgment, as well as from experiencing retaliation from the abuser.

You Might Blame Yourself
Narcissists are incredible at shifting blame onto their victim. As a result, you may have been conditioned to take responsibility for their behavior and actions. They may blame you for making them upset, for doing something you knew you "were not supposed to do," and for other reasons. This all results in you feeling like you are responsible for their actions and like you are the problem, not them. It can be a challenge for you to recognize that their behavior and actions is not your fault.

The challenge with this is that it often results in victims protecting their abusers because they do not see them as responsible for the behavior. Due to their conditioning, they begin to look at the abuser as the victim, and they feel like they are the attacker. This creates a challenging complex in their mind that presents an even more significant challenge in allowing the victim to understand the difference between reality and the falsehood they have been conditioned to believe.

You Might Feel Like You are in a Love Triangle
Triangulation is a prevalent tactic from narcissists. They do this by creating love triangles, bringing a third party into the dynamic of the relationship as a way to further terrorize you, the victim. In doing this, your abuser will promote the idea that you are "not good enough," causing you to compete for their attention and approval continually.

The person they add to the love triangle can be virtually anyone. On many occasions, this third party can be a friend of yours making things even more dramatic. It could be one of the narcissists work colleagues. You may have slight concerns about this, and they will shame you and guilt-trip you for believing that they would ever do something with another individual.

Part of being stuck in this triangle is that you, as the victim, begin to feel like you have something fundamentally wrong with you. You may start to question why your partner would show more respect and compassion toward someone else than they do toward you. This can lead to you feeling further devalued, resulting in you losing even more self-confidence and self-worth. It occurs in you blaming yourself and attempting to "fix" yourself to please the abuser, who will ultimately never be pleased.

You are Afraid of Being Successful

People who are in a relationship with a narcissist often find themselves afraid of being successful in any way. You know that your abuser has regularly punished you in the past any time you have succeeded. This stems from envy because the narcissist always wants to be the best person around and they do not appreciate when someone else has succeeded and is "outshining" them. The only time that a narcissist will seem to actually be interested in your success is when they can use it as a way to make themselves look better. For example, "My (wife/husband) achieved top rank in (her/his) career this month! I am the person with the best spouse in the room!" This allows them to take responsibility and further increase their own appearance and status as a result of your success.

Many victims find themselves having their success stolen from them as well. If you did succeed, this would mean that you would have something to be happy about that was not directly in relation to the narcissist. They could not take credit for it, nor would your sense of pride and happiness within yourself serve them. So, they steal this away from you as a way to scoop out even more of your self-worth and ability to feel pleasure. That way, you rely solely on the narcissist to be praised and celebrated. You no longer feel safe, capable, or worthy of achieving success anywhere else in your life because the narcissist has manipulated you into believing that the success or praise that you receive elsewhere is shameful and that you should only receive it from them. That way, you remain codependent and stuck in their web.

Still, you might find yourself struggling to even get that far. You may discover that you self-sabotage and refrain from achieving anything in your life for fear of having someone else punish you for your achievements. This lack of moving toward what you love or what you are passionate about often results in depression. Now, you have been isolated from loved ones, perpetually abused by someone you thought you could trust and denied the right to experience joy through the things you love and through success. It makes sense as to why you are suffering so much sadness and depression.

You Lack Self-Esteem and Self-Confidence
Whether you have yet to realize where it is coming from or you have already discovered it, virtually every single victim of narcissistic abuse has severely low self-esteem and self-confidence. This is caused by the abusive tactics of the narcissist. It starts right from the very beginning when they lure you into believing that they are incredible and wholehearted, wholesome people during the initial love-bombing. The very first time the two of you interact, they blitz you into believing that they are a great, genuine person and you fall in love with them.

The more you withstand the relationship and show that you can handle the abuse, the higher your tolerance becomes and the stronger they come down on you. The higher your tolerance for the toxic behavior, the greater the decline in your self-esteem and self-confidence, leading you into a deep and dark place where you no longer have the strength required to fight back and protect yourself. Because your own identity and sense of self-worth are so damaged, the narcissist can easily reel you in again and begin from the very beginning. They will do this over and over again, showing no true remorse or guilt for their actions, and always leading you to believe that you are the problem and that you deserve it. In all reality, you do not deserve it, you never had, and you are certainly not the one to blame. But because you have been in it for so long, you have no way of holding on to any hope that this is true and what the narcissist has told you is a lie to protect themselves and keep you trapped in the cycle.

Your Friends and Family Act Differently

A common tactic used by narcissists is called smear campaigning, which means they tell those close to you many bad things about you behind your back and twist lies to make it seem like you have changed and you are no longer a good person. They do this to manipulate people into seeing you as evil and them as good which further helps their master plan. Keeping you trapped.

As a result of the smear campaigning, you may begin to notice that your friends and family act differently around you or treat you differently from what you are used to. They may stop calling you, address you differently, or even begin to leave you out of various things intentionally. They may also not believe you when you say that you are being abused and that the narcissist has been lying to them. This can make it difficult to get help and ultimately harder to escape.

If you have noticed that your friends and family around you begin to change their behavior toward you and treat you differently, there is a good chance that this behavior is coming directly from the actions of the narcissist. Unfortunately, for many victims, this results in the narcissist having ammunition to reinforce their low self-esteem by pointing out things like "even so and so doesn't want to hang out with you anymore" or otherwise bullying you and using their changed behavior as evidence to why their words are true.

Chapter 4: The Creation of a Narcissist

In this chapter, we are going to explain how narcissistic personality disorder comes to be. This will give you some insight as to how your abuser may have gotten to where they are today. That being said, it is important to understand that most people with a narcissistic personality disorder do not believe they have anything wrong with them. Therefore they very seldom seek treatment. If they do, it will likely not be because you pressured them into it. It is suggested that you use this chapter as an opportunity to understand, rather than as a tool to attempt to show your abuser that they are abusive and to pressure them into seeking treatment.

Causes of Narcissism
The exact cause of narcissistic personality disorder is unknown. Typically, personality disorders are caused by a complex series of issues that lead to the disorder developing. It is hard to predict or determine whether a child will become a narcissist, though there are some things that are believed to contribute to the development of the disorder. Here are the three theories of what goes into the creation of a narcissist.

Theory One: Environment
The first theory involved is their environment. Psychologists and psychotherapists believe that a child's environment can contribute to the potential development of personality disorders, including narcissistic personality disorder. The primary area in the child's environment where these disorders tend to develop is directly in the parent-child relationship. Typically, excessive admiration or excessive criticism toward the child can promote the development of narcissism. If a child is raised by a parent who is a narcissist, they may also learn the behavior and begin to express themselves with narcissistic behavioral patterns. In this case, the person may be on the narcissist spectrum but may not have a full-blown narcissistic personality disorder.

Theory Two: Genetics

As with the majority of illnesses, personality disorders can be inherited by family members. If an individual has one or more people with narcissistic personality disorder in their family, they may be at a higher risk of becoming a narcissist later in their own life. Although this may be an inherited characteristic, there is no way of testing genetics to determine whether or not a person will become or is at risk of becoming a narcissist in their lifetime.

Theory Three: Neurobiology

Neurobiology refers to the connection between the brain, behavior, and thinking. Psychologists, neurologists, and other researchers believe that an individual's neurobiology may encourage them to develop narcissistic personality disorder at some point in their life. Again, there is no way to test a child's neurobiology to determine whether or not they are at risk of developing narcissistic personality disorder in their lifetime. Some theories believe that traumatic life events early in life can change the individuals' neurobiology, thus making them more likely to become a narcissist later in life. This can happen as a result of the trauma itself, or because of the way, their parents may change their behavior toward the child. For example, if the parents' divorce is traumatic to the child and the child becomes neglected by one or both parents. As a result, this can contribute to narcissism. Alternatively, if the child experienced a loss or a personal trauma, such as a serious illness or injury, and one or both parents coddled the child long after the injury attempting to protect them from further dangers, this could also contribute to the potential onset of narcissism later in life.

Risk Factors

Those who are diagnosed with narcissistic personality disorder tend to receive their diagnosis in their teens or early adulthood. That being said, many will not receive a diagnosis because they genuinely believe that there is nothing wrong with them and it is everyone else who has a problem. Despite this being the prime age for diagnosis, some children may begin to show narcissistic traits as they are growing up. Some of these may be typical to their age and will never go on to develop narcissistic personality disorder whereas other children will.

Anyone can be a narcissist, no matter what their age, gender, religion, or ethnic background may be. The disorder is not related to the demographics of the individual so much as one or a combination of the causes listed above.

The general consensus agreed upon by doctors and psychologists is that the biggest risk factor leading to the potential development of narcissism later in life is parenting. Parents who are neglectful, overindulgent, abusive or pathological have a tendency to treat their children in a way that results in the child never actually overcoming the grand sense of self that all children have. In general, children are expected to be more self-indulgent because this is how they learn about their own identity and how they fit into the world. As they grow older, this sense of self-indulgence should fade away over time as they find their answers and begin fitting in. For those who have not been raised in a household where they had access to healthy parenting, either as a result of excessive or neglectful parenting or as a result of constant traumatic abuse, they are at risk of not growing past this self-indulgent behavior. Instead, they use it as a way to feel good in spite of their parents' leading them to believe that they are unworthy of love, or as a way to continue feeling good as a result of their parents leading them to believe that they are special over everyone else and deserve to be treated as such.

Complications

There are many complications that an individual will face if they are diagnosed with narcissistic personality disorder. Of these complications, the majority of them are rooted in social behavior. Individuals with narcissistic personality disorder struggle to maintain relationships, have difficulty at work or school and may resort to drug or alcohol misuse. They are also at a higher risk for physical health problems, depression and anxiety, and suicidal thoughts or behavior. If the narcissistic personality goes untreated, and in many cases even when it is addressed, the individual may experience one or all of these symptoms. This is because, in most cases, narcissists are incapable of admitting and accepting that they are narcissistic. Doing so would result in their entire reality crashing in around them. Furthermore, transitioning from a self-serving lifestyle that others feed into as a result of their abuse and into one that requires them to think of anyone other than themselves is virtually impossible. The amount of pain and loss they would feel from this transition would be more than they are willing to endure. The only time a narcissist may actually seek support is if they have lost literally everyone in their life and they are no longer able to reel people into their abuse cycle. In this case, they may be willing to consider therapy. At that rate, therapy is not guaranteed to be effective as they may just use this as a bargaining chip to confirm that they are "doing better" when, in fact, they are not.

Another major complication that narcissists face lies in shame. As a result of their upbringing and the way they were taught, every single narcissist faces shame in their childhood. Where this shame comes from depends on what caused their narcissism in the first place, but it virtually always results in them feeling the need to "delete" their true self in favor of a false persona, which you will learn more about in Chapter 5. This behavior essentially supports the narcissist in splitting away from the aspects of themselves that they are ashamed of and supports them in creating a mask that they feel should fix what has caused the shame in the first place.

If the narcissist was raised in a neglectful household, the shame would lie within virtually every aspect of the narcissist. As a result, the repeating feeling of shame and neglect would create a sense of trauma in the child that would cause them to want to discard any aspect of themselves that brought them shame or, in their opinion, resulted in them being neglected. Their true self: the parts that they were ashamed of and that they feel lead to the neglect, would then be denied in favor of a false self or mask that would ultimately redesign their profile and make them seem likable to everyone.

If the narcissist was raised in an overly coddled household, the shame would lie within any aspect of the child that was not coddled by the parents. So, if they were deemed an academic genius, anything they struggled with that made them feel as though they were incompetent or uneducated would cause shame. They would become addicted to the praise and the attention they received when they were behaving according to their parents' standards and would feel ashamed about any aspect of themselves that did not live up to what their parents felt was acceptable. This would either be aspects of themselves that contradicted what the parents were proud of, or any aspect of themselves that were ignored or even punished out of them by the parents. The true self, then, would include all of those aspects whereas the false self would seek to discard them in favor of being entirely likable and admirable to their parents.

If the child were abused growing up, any number of aspects of themselves could bring them shame. This can be even further amplified and reinforced if the abuse experienced by the child was also narcissistic abuse. In general, these aspects will directly relate to what they felt caused the abuse. This could lead to a wide range of aspects of themselves that they would then want to discard or decimate in favor of becoming a different variation of themselves that would be void of all of the aspects that they felt lead to their abuse in the first place.

As you can see, there are many complications that can arise in the face of the shame that narcissists feel. Because they blame this part of themselves for the pain and trauma they experienced at various points in their childhood, they feel strongly about the need to hide the true self in favor of the false self, which they feel will earn them greater respect and better treatment from everyone else. Because they embody this false self entirely, this leads to their sense of believing that they are special: because in their eyes, unlike everyone else, they have worked so hard to discard the "bad" parts of who they were.

Prevention and Treatment

Preventing and treating narcissistic personality disorder is challenging since the majority of these individuals will never become properly diagnosed. If the disorder is related to parenting styles, the parent may be unwilling to admit to there being a problem as well, creating further difficulties for the child to get the required care. Still, some preventative measures and treatments are available for narcissistic personality disorder.

If you have a child with this person, you may wish to know how to prevent the disorder from developing in case they have inherited it. The best thing you can do is get treatment for any childhood mental health problems as soon as possible. You can also participate in family therapy as a way to directly support the child, as well as to learn healthy ways to communicate and cope with conflicts and emotional distress in the family. Seeking assistance from parenting classes, therapists, and social workers as needed can also support you in preventing the development of narcissistic personality disorder in your child.

The only true treatment available for narcissistic personality disorder is talk therapy. This psychotherapy strategy supports individuals in recognizing their disorder and can provide them with coping tools that allow them to lead a happier and healthier life overall. This measure does take time, however, and is not always reliable. The narcissist must be fully on board and needs to be willing to completely commit to the process to support the outcome, and even then, results are not guaranteed.

Chapter 5: False-self and True-self

If you recall from previous chapters, narcissists often lure their victims in using a mask. This mask is also called their false-self. The false self is a persona that a narcissist creates that supports them in creating a positive appearance outwardly but does not represent who they truly are inside. While those who have been abused by the narcissist may desire to see their true-self as evil and conniving, the reality is that this true-self is far more complex than that.

In this chapter, we are going to look at the differences between the false-self and the true-self of a narcissist.

The False-self

We regard the "false-self" persona daily in our lives when we look out to society and see our idols, celebrities, and other admirable figures. These individuals all have a persona that they put on for their fans, building their reputation and creating an image that others love to admire. They also have a true-self, the version of self that they share with those who are near and dear to them. The same is somewhat true with narcissists. Except that a narcissist will have a false-self that they show to everyone else and a true-self that only they know.

The false self is a mask that the narcissist creates to design the appearance of being the best. They use this false-self to construct a narrative of their life that is entirely untrue, and they use this narrative to support them in creating their ideal life. A life that is only achieved through deception, abuse, and falsehoods. The purpose of the false-self is to give others the illusion that the narcissist is somehow better than others, that they are living a fantastically grandiose life, often one that is filled with impossible claims. The false-self is constructed in such a way that supports the narcissist in divorcing their true reality and living a delusional life. Any truth that is inconvenient or that takes away from the preferred narrative of the narcissist is denied in favor of their false narrative. A true narcissist will often deny the alternative narrative – the one of the true-self – in favor of the false narrative they have created for themselves.

The narcissist, including all of their codependents, lead their lives by the same narratives. The narcissist uses this narrative to deconstruct and reconstruct the narratives of their victims, bringing them into their falsehood to live in a reality that better serves their desires and needs. Beyond the fact that this narrative is false, the biggest problem is that this narrative does not consider anyone beyond the narcissist themselves. Everyone brought into the narrative is there to serve the narcissists beliefs and views, acting as puppets in his or her storyline.

While many of us will create narratives in our own minds of how things are, this becomes a personality disorder when the narrative is only one person serving themselves through the narratives of many, or when they have become so disconnected from true reality that they become pathological, maladaptive, and dysfunctional.

Once the false-self is formed and functioning, which usually happens in the teen years or early adulthood, it essentially stifles the growth of the true-self and prevents it from operating any further. In other words, the narcissist completely integrates their false-self and completely denies their true-self. In full-blown narcissistic personality disorder, this results in the individual no longer recognizing or understanding the true-self-narrative. In fact, they will often deny that it ever existed in the first place. It appears that these individuals have zero attachment to who they truly are and live entirely in their own falsehood, deceiving themselves and everyone around them to create a life that is less painful than the one that they were originally running away from.

Narcissists often develop the false-self as a way of turning all of their best attributes into who they truly are. This may be because they were excessively admired for these in childhood, or because they were excessively punished for having flaws and so they are trying to discard their flaws entirely. This new version of themselves essentially enables the narcissist to become the person they wish they were, completely denying the person they truly are. This ensures that they no longer identify with the person they were as a child, which they felt was the cause of their parents' behaviors. For example, if a child's parents divorced and they never saw one of their parents after the divorce and felt that they were neglected, they may feel that there was something fundamentally wrong with them. As a result, they would listen for the reasons why other people praise them and begin to obsessively enhance those aspects of their personality while abandoning the aspects that they felt were not as good. This allows them to feel as though they have fundamentally changed who they are so that they are no longer the child who was abandoned for being themselves, even though that is virtually never the reason why a parent would abandon a child.

Another instance that would lead to a child wanting to develop a false-self and live in their mask permanently rather than at the rate which is normal for the average human would be if that child were repeatedly abused throughout their life. The child may then strive to change who they are to discard the aspects of themselves that they felt were responsible for them being abused. They become so good at it that they no longer believe there is anything wrong with them. They literally deny and discard all aspects of themselves that they no longer like; leading them to believe that they are truly the best person ever to have lived.

Not every narcissist will feel the need to change their mask to permanently foster the false-self as a result of attempting to get away from pain or abuse. This is only true for those who have been exposed to abuse or neglect in their childhood. For those who have been raised in an overly indulgent household where the parents coddled the child and never taught them about empathy and always lead the child to believe that they were special, can lead to an addiction. The person essentially becomes addicted to having other people swoon over their best attributes, and so they adapt to believe that they should expect this all their life. When they realize that they do not receive this treatment from others in society, they begin to act with narcissistic behaviors as a way to get it so that they can continue getting their "fix."

For narcissists, the false-self allows them the opportunity to split their personality and choose to permanently live in the narrative of one of the splits. As a result of this personality disorder being pathological, they truly can lead themselves into believing that the alternative narrative does not exist. They may even believe that it never did. This is how they protect themselves from the pain that comes from having aspects of themselves that they were never able to accept or integrate fully.

The false-self has two functions for the narcissist. First, it serves as a decoy. They use it to develop immunity to manipulation, indifference, sadism, exploitation or smothering. So, this is essentially developed by the child as a cloak to protect themselves. The second purpose of the false-self is to use it as a means to barter the way they are treated. They present the false-self as a better self, one that they believe deserves a better, painless, and more considerable treatment by others. It is used to alter others attitudes and behaviors toward the narcissist. So, not only does it protect them, but it also enables them to adjust how other people act toward them to promote a better reality for the narcissist.

Something worth noting is that even healthy individuals will have some level of a false-self. This self is a mask that they use as a persona around the world that they do not know as well. It is typically a more polished, well-created version of self that is shown to others. However, in a healthy individual, this false-self never goes beyond the false-face that they show to those they do not know very well. They continue to have a true-self that they share with family members and close friends who know who they truly are. The only time the false-self becomes a problem is when we use it to suppress who we truly are and ultimately deny entire integration, leading to us splitting off and only leading a false narrative of one aspect of our entire self.

The True-self

The true-self of a person is who they truly are inside. In the case of a narcissist, the true-self does not "die" per se, but it is completely paralyzed and incapable of being expressed by the narcissist.

The best way to understand a narcissist's true-self is to understand that this is typically their inner child. The inner child of the narcissist is often abused in a way that results in them feeling like they are not good enough or worthy enough, or that only certain aspects of themselves are lovable. This leads to the inner child feeling either completely neglected, or specific aspects of who they are being neglected.

If the child is neglected by their parents altogether, they will feel neglected, and therefore their true-self is likely an aspect of them that is filled with feelings of hurt, rejection, neglect and other forms of extremely painful psychological pain. This part of themselves is generally deeply wounded which results in them feeling the need to change who they are entirely by splitting their personality and essentially becoming a new person. By changing away from who they were when they were neglected, the narcissist attempts to become a new "superhuman" type of person who believes that, because their persona is manufactured to be the best of the best, they must be special. This results in them thinking they are better than anyone else, thus leading to the narcissist behaviors. Through this, their true-self – the wounded inner child that feels neglected and rejected – is permanently silenced and they are able to carry on living as though they are better than everyone else and deserve better treatment that results in less pain and more compassion.

If the child was heavily admired by parents, it is likely that the negative aspects of their personality were completely ignored by their parents. As a result, they were taught also to neglect and deny these aspects of self. The child would likely be heavily praised and admired for their positive actions and then would be completely neglected for negative ones. For example, if they scored high on a test, they would be admired, but if they fell off their bike, they would be ignored. This leads the child to believe that they are only worthy of love and acceptance when they are living as their best self. If the less admirable aspects of themselves, which are completely natural to all of us, are too heavily ignored while the other aspects are excessively admired, this can lead to the child believing that these aspects of themselves need to be destroyed so that they no longer experience the pain of having love or acceptance withheld.

Either way, the true-self is often highly damaged and wounded in a narcissist. They choose to deny it because, in their eyes, the true-self is responsible for attracting all of the pain and trauma unto the child. By denying this aspect of themselves and essentially destroying it and replacing it with the false-self, the narcissist can become the person that they feel is worthy of a higher degree of admiration, appreciation, acceptance, and love by others. Unfortunately, the creation and integration of the false-self lead to them not only protecting themselves from the pain of their own abuse but also results in them abusing other people in an entirely different way later in life.

The form of abuse that this leads to them casing unto others rarely looks like that which they learned in childhood unless their narcissism was a learned trait after being raised by a narcissist. The difference here is that the narcissist will generally abuse people on the pretense that they are not as good as the narcissist is and therefore they should be ashamed of themselves. Because the true self of the narcissist was never accepted and they felt it lead to so much pain, many times the narcissist grows deep, unrealized jealousy over those who live their lives genuinely *feeling* worthy as their true selves. They tend to feel angry that they were raised in a way that denied their true self when others seem to live just fine with it. As a result, they take this anger out through their abuse, destroying others' in the ways that they felt they were destroyed. In other words, because they felt that they were not allowed to be accepted for their true self, they feel that no one else should be, either.

Chapter 6: A Narcissist's Target

Narcissists, like all abusers, have a preferred "victim" that they will go after. These victims are individuals who are most likely to assimilate into the narcissist's narrative, allowing them to continue to create their own false reality. If you are in a relationship with a narcissist, you may be wondering just what initially got you into this position.

"Why me?" is a massive question that victims will ask. You may be feeling like the narcissist chose you because there is something inherently wrong with you. Alternatively, you may be feeling like there is something wrong with you because you were unable to predict the abuse and so you begin to feel ashamed in yourself. Trust that you becoming the victim is not your fault. It is not because there is anything wrong with you at all. Instead, the narcissist may have simply realized that you are highly empathetic, compassionate, and caring, and used this to exploit you into becoming another person in their falsehood reality.

Still, there are certain traits and features that all victims tend to have in common, at least to some degree. The following characteristics are the most common traits seen on the resume of a narcissists target.

Conscientiousness

One of the most overlooked qualities that a narcissists victim will portray is conscientiousness. Narcissists know that if an individual is conscientious, they are more likely to follow through on their commitments and will typically assume that the narcissist will do the same. As a result, they are able to exploit this quality to have the victim serve *them* directly.

A person who is conscientious tends to give other people the benefit of the doubt. They are more likely to grant second chances and become admissive of the narcissist's behaviors. Because this individual is already willing to give extra chances and see the good in the narcissist, the narcissist knows that they can exploit this behavior to turn a conscientious person into a pushover with an excessive need to please. If you are excessively agreeable and conscientious, you have the perfect characteristics required for a narcissist to groom you to fit their needs. They will take advantage of you, repeatedly abusing you and destroying you as you continue to choose to see the best in them. Because of your desire and need to see the good in others, you are less likely to see the narcissist for who they truly are. They thrive on this dynamic because it means that not only are you not seeing them for who they truly are, you are not even looking for it. You would rather see the good in them and give them the benefit of the doubt than admit to yourself or anyone else that they are acting out of any other reason than love or misguided attempts at showing love.

Empathy

Having empathic tendencies is a necessity if you are going to be chosen by a narcissist. They love seeing empathy in their victims because this means that you are probably extremely easy for them to manipulate. To them, this is your greatest weakness, and it will become their greatest weapon against you. Since a narcissist craves and needs attention, praise, and affirmation from others, they prey on individuals who have a high degree of empathy. These individuals are far more likely to provide the attention they need so that they can feel good.

As an empathetic person, you are more likely to be able to relate to how the other person is feeling and, as a result, you act according to what you are feeling and not necessarily what you are seeing. For a narcissist, this is a perfect dynamic. Because they are feeling a significant amount of pain and torture deep inside, they know that you can sense this and that you will take pity on them. Then, they twist that pity to get what they need out of you. They also use your empathetic side to devalue you, knowing that you are led by emotions. Those who are led by emotions tend to be easier to manipulate as all the narcissist has to do is play on your emotions by creating a sense of shame, guilt, and disappointment within you. Once they have done that, they can control when you get to feel good and when you don't.

Another great aspect of you being empathetic means that you will listen to their sob stories and feel for them. They will lie and manipulate you into believing that they are the victim, validate why, and trust that you will feel for them and that you will want to save them from being the victim. They know that you are more likely to forgive because you want to see the good in others. This only further reinforces their belief that you are not able to "think" for yourself, thus allowing the narcissist to hijack you through your emotions and force your perception to fit their needs.

If you are a highly sensitive empathetic person, often referred to as an Empath, this means that you are driven by your emotions more than the average person. Not only can you relate to what the other person is feeling, but you can genuinely feel it, too. This means that you are even more likely to take whatever they tell you and give them what they desire because you genuinely want to help them *feel* good. Only, they never will because they truly can't. As an Empath, you may be even more at risk for narcissistic abuse because of your very nature. You have a plethora of the one thing the narcissist lacks most: empathy. They flock to you like moths to a flame.

 If you believe you are an Empath and want to learn more about what this means and how you can protect yourself, you can refer to my book: *"Highly Sensitive Empaths: The Complete Survival Guide to Self-Discovery, Protection from Narcissists and Energy Vampires, and Developing the Empath Gift."*

Integrity
A morally impoverished narcissist is extremely drawn to someone who is impeccable with their word. If you have integrity, you have many attributes that a narcissist can exploit for their own personal gain. Many people who have strong integrity will not cheat on their moral code or give up on a relationship. It is easier for the narcissist to keep them trapped in the relationship until they are no longer capable of leaving because of the psychological damage that has been caused.

Narcissists feel no remorse for harming their victims. However, their victims will often feel morally apprehensive about retaliating in any way. The victim, with strong integrity, does not want to betray the relationship or step back from the obligations they feel they have to the

140

narcissist. This integrity can benefit the individual who is in a relationship with other like-minded individuals, but to one who is in a relationship with a narcissist, it can keep them trapped for years.

Resilience

An individual who is resilient is capable of enduring tough situations. The narcissist exploits the resilience of the victim in order to strengthen the bond between the victim and the abuser. This may seem counterintuitive, but it actually serves the narcissist in a big way. Individuals who are incapable of enduring the abuse are more likely to leave their relationship quite early. Those who can "toughen out" the abuse, are more likely to stay within the relationship because they heal in between incidents and can, or so they think, handle them as they happen. If the victim does leave the relationship after realizing how abusive or toxic it is, an individual with a high resiliency will bounce back during their time apart. During the hoover phase (described in detail in Chapter 7), most victims will return hoping that things will be better. If things are not better, the victim knows within that they have the strength to endure the abuse.

Resilience is a powerful quality to have that can deeply support you in overcoming adversity and achieving anything you desire in life. However, when it has been twisted around the desires of the narcissist, it can become a painful weapon that strengthens your ties to your abuser and makes you less likely to leave the relationship. A person who is resilient may be more likely to ignore their instincts to leave, choosing instead to stay and fight it out. They may adopt one of two mentalities: that of a fighter, or that of a savior. Regardless of which mentality the victim adopts, it is regularly used to attempt to sustain an unsustainable relationship.

Due to the trauma bond that the victim develops with the toxic narcissist, the victim may find themselves measuring their love by the amount of cruelty that they are willing to put up with. Sentences like "you constantly lie to me and yet I am still here, how is that not a measure of love?" may cross your mind or your lips in arguments if you are an individual with great resilience, caught in the terrifying relationship between the narcissistic abuser and victim.

141

Weak Boundaries

Individuals with already weakened boundaries are admirable to the narcissist because this means that they are easier to take advantage of and keep in their web. People who are strong in their boundaries will strong-arm the narcissist, blocking them from having the capacity to abuse them and leaving when they realize the relationship is toxic. However, those with weak boundaries already struggle to stop people from mistreating them. This means that they already have some tolerance built up for abuse, making it easier for the narcissist to pull them into the abuse cycle and keep them trapped.

If you are someone who struggles to enforce boundaries or does not recognize what healthy boundaries look like, this makes you an admirable target for the narcissist. This is even further enhanced if your weak boundaries are in direct relation to how you allow people to talk to you and treat you. If you allow people to exploit you, take advantage of you, and treat you poorly because you are unsure as to how to stop it or already feel weak against them, this means that you are already a prime candidate for abuse. Having weak boundaries can also tie in with next trait we are going to talk about; co-dependency.

Co-Dependent

Many people do not realize that they are already codependent. However, if you are already co-dependent, a narcissist will recognize this quickly and use it to their advantage. The narcissist's entire objective is to create a victim that is entirely dependent on them for virtually everything. If you are already conditioned to be codependent, this means that they do not have to condition you and it makes their job easy. Instead, they simply have to encourage you to attach yourself to them (or their web). The hardest part of their cycle is already done, making it even easier for them to hook you.

The typical tell-tale signs of codependency that narcissists will look for in potential victims include the victim messaging them first majority of the time, asking to hang-out most of the time, feeling the need to share more than seems natural for early on in a relationship, and seeking for validation and approval from the narcissist. This needy, and overly-invested behavior means that you are likely co-dependent, which makes you an easy target. The narcissist will not have to put in much work to make you become even more invested in the relationship. This also makes it easier for the narcissist to keep you stuck in their web and keep using you as narcissistic supply.

Sensitive or Passionate Romantic

People who identify as sensitive or as passionate romantics are preferred by the narcissist. These individuals are easily swooned by the love-bombing phase, which helps the narcissist hook them in and keep them invested in the relationship. Because very few people are as intensely romantic as the passionate romantic identifies as, and even fewer are perfectly curated for the individual, this makes them easier targets. The narcissist can easily look into what makes you feel loved, how they can romance you, and what it would take to sweep you off your feet. Then, they tailor the love-bombing phase to you. Through this ability to curate the perfect love-filled scenario for you, the narcissist is easily able to hook you in.

Because you are a sensitive individual, this also means that you take heartbreak and pain harder than the average person. The narcissist is aware of this and knows that it will be even harder for you to leave them compared to the average individual. As long as they make the pain of leaving more than you can bear to endure, they can feel confident that you will not be going anywhere any time soon. And as a result, they gain even more power over you and can keep using you as narcissistic supply.

Sentimentality

Another thing that narcissists prefer in individuals is a high degree of sentimentality. People who are more likely to love deeply are more likely to bond quickly and deeply with the narcissist, making their abuser-victim relationship strong. Narcissists will generally love-bomb their victim, appealing to their desire to have a strong and deep relationship with their lover. This is how they lure them in during the early stages of the relationship. This enables the narcissist to secure the love, trust, and commitment of the individual early on.

The narcissist will exploit the individual's sentimentality to create pleasurable memories that the victim will romanticize and hold onto during periods where the abuse takes place. This encourages them to see the good in the narcissist, resulting in them being more likely to forgive their abuse and see it as a bad day or a mistake.

Once the individual has committed and is deeply in love with the narcissist, the narcissist will begin to withhold emotions and withdraw as a way to create feelings of emotional depletion in their victim. Then, the victim begins to scramble to hold on and make things "better." They are more likely to rationalize and justify the behavior, omit it from punishment, and protect the abuser if the victim is first filled with love and positive memories to hold onto.

The Recipe of the Perfect Target

An individual who possesses all or most of the traits listed above is a perfect target for a narcissist to latch onto and exploit for their own sick games. These characteristics all work together to design an individual who is susceptible to being abused and staying in the cycle. They are more likely to forgive and move past the abuse, they are easier to form deep bonds with, and they are capable of continuing to love the narcissist and fulfill their need for love, attention, acceptance, and praise.

If you possess these traits, there is a good chance that they were exploited to being used against you. Sadly, most of these traits are positive traits for any individual to carry. When they are used in a healthy setting, they support you in leading a highly connected, successful, thriving life that can have positive outcomes. When exploited by an abuser, however, they can quickly become weapons that are used against you.

Instead of creating a positive connection they are used to design a forced connection with the narcissist. Instead of encouraging success, they are used to devalue you and prevent you from creating any level of achievement in your life. Instead of providing you with the ability to thrive, they are used to suck the life out of you. Narcissists are highly powerful at using your best traits and characteristics to turn them into your worst nightmares. This is what makes them so powerful. They are sneaky about it, and they will play you in all of the right ways to keep you hooked and coming back for more.

Please, do not let this information dishearten you in any way. Remember, awareness is the first step to escaping the narcissist and beginning your road to recovery.

Chapter 7: The Abuse Cycle

The narcissistic abuse cycle is somewhat straightforward, but also extremely complex. While writing it out on paper is fairly easy, the execution of it is challenging. Being on the victim side is even more difficult as you are regularly blindsided by the cycle, often to the point that you do not see it happening at all. It may take many experiences of the cycle, maybe even years of being trapped in it before you actually see what is happening. Even then, it often goes on for a long time before the victim is finally able to walk away for good.

Being able to recognize and leave the abuse cycle is extremely challenging for a victim because they are constantly battling between emotions and logic, reality and fantasy. Emotions are what hook them in, to begin with: the deep passion, the intense feelings, and the love for the narcissist. However, as they begin to see the narcissist's mask slip from time to time, their logical mind begins to kick in. This can lead to you doubting the validity of your emotions and wondering if it is all just a lie, or if your emotions are telling the truth. However, because they are so strong and intoxicating from the narcissist's abuse, most victims who begin to hear the voice of logic will just as quickly silence it in favor of their addiction to the moments of praise and pleasure they receive from the love-bombing phase with the narcissist.

Many times, victims know that the narcissist is abusive or toxic because their logical mind can identify it. As a result of their emotions, however, the victim doubts this reality and keeps themselves entrapped in the relationship by following their heart and avoiding pain, rather than seeing the situation for what it truly is and finding safety outside of it. Especially if the victim has high traits of co-dependency, the alternative option of leaving can seem just as painful, leaving the victim in a catch-22 or in other words, stuck.

This chapter is going to give us the opportunity to explore the abuse cycle itself in an in-depth manner, as well as the different styles of abuse that are employed by the narcissist to create the desired effect. This will support you in recognizing how it happens, as well as understanding the specific tools that your abuser is using to facilitate the abuse.

Outline of the Abuse-Cycle

Before we get into detail on the cycle itself, you must know the outline. I also want you to know that reading this may be challenging if you are just beginning to realize that you are in a relationship with a narcissist. If that is the case, take your time and go easy on yourself. You have already begun the healing process.

The outline of the cycle of abuse that victims experience by their narcissist contains 5 phases. These 5 phases are:

- Idealization
- Devaluation
- Discarding
- Destroying
- and Hoovering

The Abuse Cycle

The following five steps are all a part of the narcissistic cycle of abuse. These happen in virtually every single cycle, so it is important to be cautious and aware. If you are a victim, pay attention to these cycles so that you can begin to witness them as they happen. This will support you in having a greater understanding of your abuser, seeing the reality behind what they are doing and giving you the power to leave.

Idealize

The process of idealizing allows the narcissist to make themselves appear better than what they really are. During this stage, they often do what we call love-bombing. This means that the narcissist starts creating an ideal relationship for you by showing you massive amounts of interest, love, and affection. This leads to you developing a deep sense of trust toward the narcissist, helping you to connect with them on a deeper level. Or, so you think. You share many things with them, letting them know about your deepest secrets, hopes, and fears. They share information with you, too, though it is rarely genuine. In many cases, it may not even be the truth.

The narcissist will continue to string you on for a while, making the relationship seem almost too-good-to-be-true, but never letting the other shoe drop. At least, not until it is the right time to do so. Instead, they let you grow deeply comfortable with them. They give you enough time to develop strong feelings for them and to see what a great person they are. Or, what a great person they want you to *think* they are. The connection and ecstasy shared between you two is simply amazing. You can't believe you have met someone you can connect with on a deeper level mixed with explosive physical chemistry. You can't get enough.

For the narcissist, this phase is all about collecting data. Everything you are sharing with them is being stored away to be later used against you during the phase of devaluation. They want to create a secure environment for you so that you feel like they have everything you want, and they want to know everything about you, so they can use it against you in the future. Once they've got you hooked, they know that you will do anything to protect the relationship. For the narcissist, this is the key step for them being able to keep you attached to them for as long as possible.

Devalue

Once the narcissist is confident they have hooked you significantly, and you are heavily invested in the relationship, the narcissist will then start to move into the devaluation phase. This is where they begin to chip away at you and shift your perception so that your strengths now appear as flaws. The process of switching from idealization to devaluation is slow. At first, you won't even recognize it because it is so subtle. They intentionally bring it out very carefully, increasing your tolerance for their abuse as they go along. They may start out with all pull and no push, reeling you in and keeping you coming back for more. Over time, however, this begins to change. Soon, there will be 10% push, then 20%, then 30% and so on and so forth until the entire relationship is filled with majority abuse and toxicity. The gradual increase takes months, even years to reach maximum capacity. The length of time it can take and the amount of pressure put on the victim all depend on the signals you are giving off and your level of tolerance. The narcissist wants to know that they are winning, and they want to feel confident that you are giving up. If you have stronger boundaries going into the relationship or you demand that the relationship starts at an even 50:50 for power and control, they will continue to apply the amount of pressure that you can handle without recognizing what is going on until they win.

At that point, however, you are the frog in boiling water. They have conditioned you by building up your tolerance over a long period of time, and you didn't even see it coming because of how gradually it happened. If the narcissist was to do it any other way, you would see the abuse and leave. So, they strategically measure out only what you can handle and continue pushing more and more. They may have to throw you a bone every so often and give you some pull in the form of flattery or affection. The main goal is to shift the ratio to majority negativity and build up your level of tolerance, chipping away at your self-worth more and more. As your level of tolerance towards the abuse grows, it becomes harder for you to leave.

Once the narcissist feels that they have reached a high enough push/pull ratio, they know they have reached a state of control. Here, they feel powerful over the relationship, and they begin to get worse and worse.

They begin to take advantage of the fact that they are now in control and the pressure becomes even greater, perhaps causing the ratio to increase far quicker now that they know you will not leave. During this part of the process, they will also be targeting other potential victims to attempt to lure them in. This way, when they reach the devaluation phase with you, they can begin getting attention from someone else. This keeps them in the constant state of receiving attention, yet perfectly grooming everyone else to give it to them.

The devaluation phase of the process is very painful and traumatic to the victim. If you were once known to be confident and sexy, they would now push you into believing that you are actually cocky and vain. If you were once intelligent, you are now a know-it-all. They use the devaluation phase to gaslight you, invalidating your feelings and beliefs and abusing you into believing an alternate reality that is far from the truth. Here, you begin to have your self-image, and self-worthiness cut down. Your successes begin to mean nothing as they discourage you and fill you with doubt, fear, and insecurity. They use the devaluation phase to prevent you from creating future success, as well as to create deep insecurity that causes you to feel like you are incapable of escaping. This part of the abuse cycle can be highly traumatizing as the narcissist will seek to destroy you in every way possible.

During the devaluation phase, the majority of victims have no idea what they are actually experiencing. They do not know what they are going through. Victims are entangled in a web that is spun by the narcissist and, often, they have no idea that they are even in it. It is extremely painful when in this stage. The heart-breaking thing is the victim will do everything to fight to get back to the initial love-bombing phase of affection, chemistry, connection, ecstasy, and love. But it is too late. This is exactly where the narcissist wants you.

From here, the narcissist will do one of two things. If they are not yet certain about where you stand and how deep you are in the hole, they will move back and forth between the idealization and devaluation phase. Each time, the devaluation phase will grow longer and longer, until eventually, you are here almost permanently. At that point, you will only be entered into the idealization phase as rewards for your behavior if they feel that you deserve it. That way, they continue to give you small reasons to stay with them, which you will cling to as a result of your internal emotional and mental destruction. This enforces your codependency on them and allows them to slowly but consistently hack into your self-confidence, self-esteem, and self-worth. At this point, you are still desperately clinging onto the initial love-bombing phase and the idea of leaving the relationship is more painful than tolerating the abuse. Once they are confident that you are officially hooked and that they can treat you in any way they want, they will begin including the discard phase.

Discard
During your desperate attempts to get back to the initial phase that felt so good, the narcissist will discard you. Because you are now feeling deeply insecure and insignificant, they know that you will do anything to seek their approval. This essentially conditions you to seek excessive admiration from the narcissist, putting the power directly in their hands. Now, they use your need for validation to support their own agenda. They will frequently withdraw, telling you that everything you have done for them is a sign of failure, and blaming you for not making them feel "good." That way, you begin to blame yourself. As you continue to seek validation desperately, they use all of your attempts as a way to feed and fuel their own need for validation, attention, praise, and admiration. In other words, you are feeding the fire.

This behavior supports the narcissist in scooping out all of the remaining qualities within you that do not serve their agenda. At this point, they know that you are so desperate for their attention and affection that you will do nearly anything to win it back. So, they scoop away. They know that there is a good chance that you have not even yet begun to realize how minimal your self-esteem and self-worth has gotten because the devaluation has been so slow and gradual. To them, this means that you are oblivious to what is keeping you attached, which means there is little chance that you can or will break the attachment. You may grow frustrated and leave for some time, but this rarely lasts. You would first have to recognize what was going on and then receive help to leave the situation permanently, which is an unlikely scenario for most victims.

At this point, nothing you can do will fill their high standards. They set their standards higher and higher, continually putting them out of reach so that you cannot possibly achieve them. As the blame shifting continues, they will use your desperation and confusion as an opportunity to turn themselves into the victim. Often, they will blame you for stuff that they have done themselves and then delude you into believing that it was you who actually did it.

As this is all happening, the narcissist will be bringing other people into the dynamic. During your time apart, they will bond with other victims to fill their needs and create a love-bombing phase. In their mind, they are creating back-up plans of narcissistic supply just in case you do manage to escape forever. The narcissist cannot cope alone. When you get back together with the narcissist, they will claim that this person is close to them but that it has no impact on your relationship. They will then successfully keep two or more of you trapped in this cycle, constantly switching between which one has the "pleasure" of filling their needs. The narcissist will rarely if ever, spend any time alone during these discard phases. Even being alone for as little as a few nights is plenty enough time for triangulation to root in deeply and start, especially because the narcissist has already been priming their next victim since the devaluation in most phases.

In some cases, victims will leave the narcissist first. Rather than waiting for the discard phase to begin, they take the cue and choose to leave on their own. This can happen in some cases because they do not understand why the narcissist is treating them so poorly and they are struggling to find any reason to stay. So, the victim threatens to leave. If the victim does not leave, this will only further anchor in the narcissist's attempts to devalue their victim. If the victim does leave, they will not be gone long before the hoover phase starts. Through the hoover phase, the narcissist harasses the victim until they willingly give the narcissist attention once again. Then, the idealization phase starts once more so that the narcissist can re-hook the victim and bring them back into the cycle. The more the hoover phase is successful, and the victim is lured back, the stronger the hook grows and the harder it is for the victim to endure the discard phase when it inevitably arises once more.

Destroy

At this point, there is a strong possibility that the relationships the narcissist has been working on behind the scenes with other victims have now become more developed. The narcissist now has more sources of narcissistic supply and is less dependent on you. This is where the destroy phase starts to begin.

During the destroy phase, the narcissist will continue to pressure you into taking the blame. They will then dig deeper into a devaluation process, using your weakness and vulnerability as an opportunity to really drive their abuse deep. They will often switch back and forth between the two phases, making you feel worthless and causing it to seem like if you leave you will have nowhere to go and no one to turn to because you are not worthy of anyone's care or love. They will also make it seem like you have no other choice but to leave because you are no longer welcomed to stay with them.

Here, they will use all of your insecurities against you. Everything they learned about you during the idealization phase will come back to haunt you as they twist it deep, causing you to doubt yourself and to see your strengths as your biggest flaws, leaving you to feel like you have nothing left to offer. If they know that you are afraid of being seen as needy, for example, they will use your desperate attempts to seek validation as a way to amplify this insecurity and peg you as excessively needy. They will exploit all of your insecurities, fears, and elements of your past to cause you to feel completely unworthy.

Here, you begin to believe them. Your spirit is crushed, your hope is destroyed. You begin to feel as though they are your only cure and you *need* them to undo what they have done. For that reason, you continue to try to seek their validation and do everything that you can to have them accept you and "make everything better." Now, you no longer have the strength to walk away, nor do you feel like you can undo the world of hurt and pain they have caused within you. You seek to them as your remedy, though you may also begin to withdraw for fear of being lashed out at and hurt again. You are likely left in this uncomfortable phase of needing their validation but feeling too hurt to talk to them or seek it any further. You are destroyed. Your energy is depleted, and you no longer have what it takes to continue fighting. To the narcissist, you are like a tired prey who have ended their running and is ready to roll over and admit defeat.

During the destroy phase, the narcissist will go to any great length to ensure that you feel completely unworthy and unwanted. They will say things like "No wonder your mother doesn't like having you over anymore" or "This is why your friends don't hang out with you anymore" to make you feel like you have nowhere left to turn. In reality, the narcissist is the direct reason why these individuals no longer see you as often.

Other things the narcissist may say during the discard phase include things like: "I never loved you," "I can't believe you thought I would care about you," "Your boyfriend from the eleventh grade was right, you are fat and worthless," or anything else they can draw on to make you feel like you have nothing. They want to take everything away from you, leaving you feeling like you are stranded on an island. Because they back everything up with painful evidence from your life,

154

stuff that you have confided in them previously, they can easily manipulate your emotions to leave you feeling like they are right. Now, the only thing left for you to do is beg for forgiveness for something you never did or leave and attempt to regain everything you lost.

Hoover

Once the destroy phase is over, you and the narcissist will most likely spend some time away from each other. You may have escaped yourself or the narcissist may have temporarily abandoned you. If you are coming out of the destroy phase for the first time, you can be sure it is not over. While the narcissist will have their other victims beginning their abuse-cycle phase, you will be put into the hoovering phase. The narcissist likes to have back-up plans.

The hoover phase is actually where the majority of the trauma will occur, despite the rest of the cycle being exhausting and traumatic as well. Here, victims typically cannot fight their addiction or need for validation. Some might escape for a few weeks or even months, but most will return in the end. No matter how hard they try, their life always seems to feel empty without the narcissist because they are no longer being used and abused in the way that they have been conditioned to. The narcissist has expertly conditioned them into needing this abusive situation, making them eager to come back to the narcissist for more. Despite it being a long time, the victim also still will endlessly crave the initial idealization phase. That is unless they have adequate support in leaving the situation and are able to seek assistance in staying away.

Soon, the victim begins to idealize the relationship in their own mind. They miss the narcissist, so they begin ignoring all of the bad and negative experiences in favor of the ones that brought them joy. They romanticize the idealization phase and minimize the rest. After enough time passes, the narcissist knows that the victim will begin downplaying the abuse or even going so far as to believe that it was barely abusive, to begin with. Many times, they will think if they were to do things differently, then the relationship would have been better. This leads to them longing to have the relationship back.

In the meantime, the victim finds it to be quite challenging to assimilate in the normal world. Their independence is challenging to get back, they rarely have any confidence, and it is challenging for them to get into any further relationships because they simply do not feel as though are good enough for anyone else and able to trust anyone. The words of the narcissist ring through their minds, reminding them to feel that they are not worthy of the love or affection of anyone. As a result of the abuse and the destruction of their self-esteem and self-confidence, the victim will now also likely begin experiencing self-sabotaging behaviors that further minimize their sense of self-worth. These behaviors will not necessarily be related to dating or relationships, either. Some self-sabotaging behaviors that are common in victims during the hoover phase include things like overeating, sleeping too frequently, giving up on exercise, not engaging in social activities or anything else that keeps them from re-entering normal life as they knew it before the narcissist. The victim will often find themselves feeling lonely and unhappy, and they begin to feel like they need the narcissist back just to defeat the loneliness. They may begin to idealize again in their own minds, which leads them back to the narcissist where it starts all over in the idealization phase.

During this phase, the narcissist will also regularly make attempts to reconnect with the victim. These attempts will most likely be made when they are not receiving attention anywhere else, thus resulting in them needing a fix. Chances are, they are connecting with other victims at the same time, seeing who will fill their needs first and in the most effective way possible. The messages will often start with a simple "Hey" sent to the victim's phone or inbox. Then, it will move on to messages that are used to lead the victim into believing that the narcissist sees what they have done wrong and that they will not do it again. Small attempts of love-bombing and idealization will occur. For example, messaging the victim a text like "Hey cutie, how are you? I miss you terribly."

Through the conversations, the narcissist sets the belief that they will be better again and that this relationship will be the way it was during the idealization phase. This plays into the victim's hope that things could be better if they were to act differently and certain things were changed this time around. The narcissist plays on this belief, leading the victim to feeling confident that it would be better if they were to try again. This, however, is untrue. The narcissist has no intention of being kind or compassionate, however. Instead, they will remain the abuser, and the victim will remain the victim. What is actually happening here is a power dynamic, where the narcissist is luring their victim back and getting an ego boost by knowing that they can go back to their "old supply." This is essential for you as the victim to understand: the narcissist *will not be any different.* Even if they revisit the idealization phase to bring you back, they are still abusive, and they will still devalue, discard, and destroy you. This is likely to happen several times over and over again, sometimes tens or even dozens of times before the victim ever understands what is going on. In some cases, the victim never will, and they will live out their entire life being lured back and forth by the abuse of the narcissist. Eventually, it happens so often that the narcissist barely even makes an attempt to hide themselves or their intentions anymore. They are so confident that you will come back that they simply wait for you to come back on your own, or they make futile attempts to lure you back in if they feel you do not come back quickly enough.

If you do not give in to the attempts of the narcissist when they begin trying to reconnect, they will often begin attempting to punish you as a way to lure you back. They will start using smear campaigns, lying to those in your life or anyone who will listen to them to lead them into believing that you are a bad person or that you are someone who they shouldn't associate with anymore. These smear campaigns are often done in an effort to isolate you, pushing you to feel lonely so that you will message them back. They know that if you have no one and they approach you with a promise of love and affection that you are more likely to respond to them. So, they will do anything it takes to get you into that state that will surely leave you wanting to come back to them. In their eyes, they want you to behave as they have trained you to even when you are no longer together. In your eyes, you have nowhere else to turn.

Cycle Symptoms for the Victim

The previous steps were the abuse cycle that you will experience step-by-step with the narcissist. However, there is also a victim cycle. This cycle is perpetuated by the abuse and is the cycle that the abuser wants you to become trapped in. They want you to continually move back and forth between these two stages: cognitive dissonance and codependency. That is how they keep you weak and returning for more.

Cognitive Dissonance

The first stage of the cycle for the victim is cognitive dissonance. Cognitive dissonance is the mental pain and discomfort experienced when a new contradictory belief clashes with an original belief, by some new evidence. After being under a false belief about someone for quite some time and then having that belief gradually peeled away as they expose who they truly are, can be excruciatingly painful. Not only is it painful, but it is also immensely overwhelming and very hard to accept as a new reality. Especially when there is so much emotion attached to the original belief.

In healthy scenarios, cognitive dissonance is an opportunity to learn more about ourselves and correct our beliefs and behaviors. In unhealthy scenarios, such as with abuse, cognitive dissonance can be

158

far too painful for the victim, that you refuse to change your beliefs despite witnessing new evidence. Even though logic may serve in showing that your original beliefs and emotions towards the narcissists were incorrect, it is very difficult to override your original beliefs because of the sheer pain and tragedy that would arise from this experience. For many, it is too much to bear and keeps the victim trapped in the narcissist's web.

This battle of cognitive dissonance within the mind of the victim can go on for months or even years. As the abuse from the narcissists continues to grow, and their mask gradually slips bit by bit, the victim receives more and more new evidence contrary to their original beliefs about the narcissist. As difficult as it is, the victim needs to detach from their original beliefs about the narcissist in order to free themselves.

Co-dependency

Once the narcissist has given the victim a glimpse of their true-self behind the mask in the de-value phase, the victim will fight to get back to the idealize phase. When this occurs, the narcissist will use this to their advantage and drive you into a state of co-dependency. This is the part of the greater cycle where you begin to desperately seek validation and affection, and they proceed to the discard and destroy phases. Because they are in the power position here, they can pressure you into feeling like you are incapable of doing anything and you *need* them to support you in becoming capable. The narcissistic abuser wants you to feel like they are your lifeline and you are unable to achieve, do, or be anything without them. This is how they ensure that you are going to come back for more.

When you are abused into a state of co-dependency, it can feel like you are unable to step away on your own. They have you exactly where they want you at this point. You feel incomplete, and they are the "missing piece," and so you will always come back for more. Co-dependency as a result of abuse is a psychological disorder that is rooted deeper every time the cycle is completed, and you are scrambling for their validation and acceptance. Unraveling it and realizing that you are capable of being whole and independent on your own is a challenging process that, in most cases, requires a professional support system to help you untangle yourself from the web.

You can often tell you are co-dependent by looking for one key change in your behavior: where your needs lie. If you feel that you need the other person to make you feel happy, like you have nothing without them, or like you require their validation to make decisions in your life, there is a good chance that you are experiencing co-dependency.

If you are experiencing co-dependency in your relationship, it is important that you take the measures to heal this through therapy following the termination of the relationship with the narcissist. Co-dependency can carry on into other relationships going forward, often sabotaging otherwise healthy relationships or worse: lead you directly to another narcissist. Getting proper help can support you in making sure this does not carry on and that you are not further harmed by the narcissist going forward.

Feeling Guilty
A state that is often felt by the victim of abuse is a deep feeling of guilt. When the narcissist manipulates you, they lead you to believe that you are the one in the wrong. They use evidence from your time spent together and from your past to validate why you are the attacker and why they are the victim. You are manipulated into feeling guilty for supposedly hurting them. You may even find yourself taking responsibility for the downfall of the relationship, feeling like it was your fault that you had a falling out and the narcissist never did anything wrong. If you do still see the wrongdoings that they have done, you will likely justify them by believing that they were only done in response to what you had initially done to them.

The reality is that you never actually did anything to earn the abuse, nor did you even instigate the falling out in the first place. Instead, this is another symptom of the narcissist successfully abusing you and manipulating you into seeing them as the one who needs attention and care. This way, they do not have to admit to doing anything wrong, nor do they have any reason to apologize. You, however, feel like you must do far more than what is reasonable to receive their forgiveness. This is where they get plenty of attention to fill the needs that they felt were not being met, which likely caused them to instigate the initial arguments in the first place.

Fear of Being Alone

Many victims find themselves fearing loneliness. Because you have been repeatedly told that you are worthless and no one would ever love you, you quickly find yourself fearing loneliness. This happens in two ways.

In the bigger picture, you are afraid of being left by yourself and never finding love again. So, you cling to your relationship with the narcissist to avoid an extremely lonely fate. The narcissist purposefully instills this phase, knowing that this will decrease your chances of escaping.

In your day-to-day life, this may even manifest as a fear of being alone even for a short period of time. You may feel like whenever you are alone, you could easily be abandoned or neglected. You may also begin to sit with your thoughts and realize how toxic the relationship is and then begin feeling immense pain for these realizations. Alternatively, you may sit by yourself with the intense fear that the narcissist is cheating on you or spending time with one of the people whom they have brought in for the purpose of triangulation, rather than doing what they have actually said they are doing.

Fear of The Truth

While some victims of narcissism will be hungry for the truth, others may actually fear knowing it. This ties in with the battle of cognitive dissonance we mentioned earlier. Although the facts may be clearly there, it can be easier for the victim to 'turn a blind eye' and cling to their original beliefs during the love-bombing phase. Learning the truth could affirm many painful pieces of information to the victim that can lead to deep feelings of embarrassment, heartbreak, and shame.

For example, perhaps learning the truth confirms that they have indeed let someone else lie to them, exploit them, and abuse them for however long the relationship with the narcissist lasted. Perhaps learning the truth confirms that the narcissist has been cheating on the victim for however long. This can be painful to admit that you would allow such a thing to happen in your life. In reality, the victim has only allowed it to happen because they had no idea that it was actively happening.

It is important to note, that after a lot of time and pain has passed, some victims will no longer want to avoid the truth. Some will actively seek out the truth despite how painful it may be, especially following the end of the relationship. There comes a point where knowing the truth helps the victim understand the reality of the relationship and can support them in escaping the narcissist and staying away. The more they know, the more evidence they have that the relationship is toxic and will not change and therefore it gives them even more reason to believe that the relationship will continue to be painful and harmful.

Chapter 8: Escaping and Healing

Escaping and healing from a narcissistic relationship is one of the most challenging things that we can do. There are many things emotionally and psychologically that keep us trapped in the relationship. Some victims may fear being physically abused by the narcissist as well. Having the ability to break the trauma bond, safely escape, regain your independence and heal the trauma is essential but challenging.

Breaking the Trauma Bond

One of the biggest reasons why it is such a challenge to escape from a relationship with a narcissist is because the victim forms a trauma bond with the narcissist. Trauma bonding is a form of strong emotional attachment that an abused person forms between his or her abuser. It is perpetuated by the cycle of abuse and reinforced each time the abuse-cycle is successfully completed. While bonding in and of itself is natural and healthy under the right circumstances, bonds developed in the process of abuse are unhealthy and traumatic to the victim. People who have grown up in abusive households are more likely to develop these bonds with multiple people because, to them, this is a "normal" bond to have.

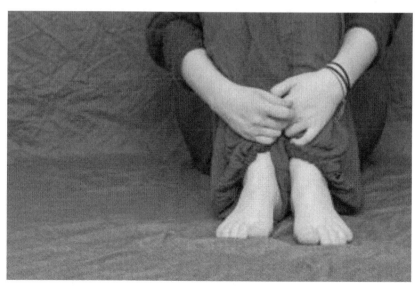

In addition to the trauma bond itself, there is also damage that occurs within the brain when we are exposed to abuse for a long period of time. When you have been abused, you will likely suffer from some degree of Complex Post-Traumatic Stress Disorder (CPTSD). CPTSD is a psychological condition that is stored in various places throughout the brain, making it challenging to release and eliminate. This disorder will actually rewire your brain, causing you to chronically live in a state of fight or flight. While you can still resume a relatively normal life following the breaking of the relationship and abuse cycles, if CPTSD is not properly healed you will carry it with you for life. Because it will rewire your brain, you will essentially train yourself to live around the symptoms of CPTSD, which can result in you losing your quality of life and feeling like you are trapped even long after the break.

Breaking the trauma bond is an essential part of leaving your abusive relationship. It can be a challenge, but it is possible. The first step is to consciously decide that you want to live in reality and not within the falsehood of the abuse. It starts with confronting all of the denials and illusions that you have lived in, including the ones the abuser made for you and the ones you made for yourself. It is essential that you realize that this person is abusive and will never change. Of course, it is okay to grieve this as it truly does feel like a real loss. You are losing a person whom you thought you had, but you never truly did.

In addition to choosing to consciously live in reality, you need to create boundaries. There should be a no-contact boundary between you and your abuser. You do not contact them, ever. If for some reason you must keep them around, such as if you share custody of children, minimize the contact and keep it very focused on necessary topics and nothing else. Breaking your habits and changing these patterns can be a challenge, but they are necessary. It can be extremely helpful to seek external support to assist you in relieving yourself from the trauma bond, and other aspects of trauma that linger in your brain. Healing does take time and having professional support is extremely beneficial for your long-term health. Be sure always to choose a therapist who is trauma-informed, so they genuinely understand what you are going through and what you need.

You should also understand that breaking trauma bonds takes time. Be gentle and patient with yourself. Remember, the creation of the bond itself was not overnight. It took time to build so it will take time to unravel and eliminate as well. Stay intentional and focused but be patient with yourself and all of the challenges that you may face in the process.

Escaping Safely

The very first thing you absolutely must know before leaving a relationship with a narcissist is that they *will* continue to try and manipulate you. They will pressure you into believing that you are overreacting, blame you for everything that happened, and attempt to con you into believing that they genuinely miss you and that they want you back. An abuser will always make false promises of a better future to draw their victims back in. It is essential to understand that you cannot trust anything they say, ever. Anything they attempt to do is in an effort to manipulate you back into the relationship. You must try to look at the bigger picture and understand the narcissists end goal. It may take you a few rounds of the entire abuse-cycle before you finally realize.

It is also essential that you leave cold turkey and allow yourself to endure the pain that comes with it. You may feel as though you are unable to, but trust that you can. Again, seeking support from understanding loved ones and trained therapists can be incredibly helpful at this point. Instead of contacting the narcissist in a moment of weakness, contact a loved one or a professional instead.

The Extreme Importance of No Contact

To successfully escape and stay away from the narcissist, you *must* enforce 'No-Contact.' If you feel that you are in serious danger from this person, having a legally enforced law surrounding the No-Contact order may be required to ensure that you have the support of law enforcement in this clause.

If you have any contact with the narcissist whatsoever, you are giving them easy access to manipulate you and keep you in the relationship longer. No matter what you think, this will be true. Any time you communicate with the narcissist, every single piece of communication will be designed to manipulate you and lure you back in. If you communicate with the narcissist, you are allowing your own mind to justify and rationalize why it may be a good idea to go back to the narcissist. You have to realize you are in a very vulnerable and weak position at this moment of time. You must vanish from the narcissist and focus on your recovery. You have to refrain from contacting them for any reason whatsoever, unless it is absolutely mandatory (such as if you share children with them.) And even if you do share children, you must work towards creating an understood schedule between both parties, where no communication (or very minimal) is needed.

Whenever the narcissist begins the hoover phase and starts trying to lure you back in, you must also understand that they are doing so only because they are lonely and they want to exploit you for their own needs. There is nothing genuine here. They do not miss you, love you, or need you in their life no matter what they say. This can be extremely challenging to understand and to embrace on an emotional level, especially because of how you have been abused and lead on by the narcissist. Because of the number of emotions that may arise any time you feel the need to contact them, or anytime they contact you, having a trauma-informed therapist and empathetic friends or family members that you can turn to during these times will be extremely supportive in helping you stay away from the narcissist.

Realize that no matter how good your intentions are in leaving the relationship, you will have to fight temptation. It is very easy for your mind to replay the good times from the relationship and to convince yourself that things may be different the next time you go back. Many victims will leave the relationship with no intention to go back, only to be lured back in *dozens* of times before hopefully realizing that things will never change. This is because you have a trauma bond, which keeps you seeing the "good" in this person and justifying your return. What you are actually seeing are the lies and manipulation, but as a victim, it can be extremely challenging to decipher the difference. This is because it would require you to admit and endure the reality that *every* aspect of the relationship was a self-serving lie fed to you by the narcissist. Which, understandably, is extremely challenging for anyone to admit, let alone endure the aftermath of the admission. This aspect can lead to complex PTSD, that makes it mentally devastating for any victim to attempt to endure or leave.

Another reason why your No-Contact order is absolutely necessary is that the hoover and idealization phases are so well-refined with a narcissist, and you are already so mentally destroyed from the CPTSD and trauma bond, that there is virtually no other way to overcome this aspect than to seek professional support and break contact. As a victim, you have become addicted to the idealization phase. What leads you back and causes you to justify the rekindling of the relationship is generally the fact that you desperately want to have that deep, passionate, tailor-made love once again. It is something that is rare to find in organic relationships, thus meaning that you have likely never experienced anything like it. It gives your mind a high with the hormones of dopamine and serotonin that actually physically leaves you addicted to this phase. You become so addicted to it that, like anyone addicted to anything else, you easily overlook the dangerous and damaging parts of the addiction in favor of your "fix." This only further supports the narcissist's hoover phase, which ultimately leads to a relapse every single time.

When leaving the relationship with a narcissist, ensure your physical safety and maintain *absolutely no-contact*. I cannot stress this enough. During this time, you will be extremely vulnerable to "relapse" into the addictions of the relationship and the only way that you can completely avoid this is by quitting the relationship cold turkey and never looking back.

Healing from Your Narcissistic Relationship
The healing process is not fixed within any particular time frame. How long it takes varies from one person to the next. There are many things that you can do to promote healing, however. The following practices will help you hugely with healing yourself and healing the trauma within your brain. It is important to understand that healing trauma in

your brain is a lengthy and challenging process and that it is best not to do it alone. Seeking support is always the answer, and it is also essential to make sure that the support is empathetic, caring, and genuinely invested in your healing. You are vulnerable at this time, so be cautious not to jump into another abusive situation when seeking support.

Having boundaries is essential. You should begin practicing boundaries with yourself and with other people around you. When you have been abused by a narcissist, boundaries are something you have been conditioned to eliminate so that you can be fully available to the abuser. It is time to start practicing saying no and being very choosy about who you let into your life. Be picky with the energy that you let into your life.

You need to spend some time eliminating the toxicity from your life. Since you have been very isolated during this experience, externalizing can be helpful. Practice journaling, speaking your truth, and talking to a trusted loved one. Getting out everything you have been holding in can be very therapeutic in helping you release everything built up inside of you and moving on.

After a long time of lies, it is essential that you take this time, to be honest with yourself. As well, you need to forgive yourself. Realizing that part of you knew and forgiving yourself for knowing but not feeling strong enough to do anything about it is essential. You should also forgive yourself for anything you hold against yourself regarding your relationship. Trust that if you could have done better, you would have done better. Abuse can be tricky, and you are the victim, not the abuser.

Doing the deep work is important. When we are abused, we carry a lot of damage within us. This is where you are going to get to work through your inner trauma and heal everything inside of you. Spend time going through the pieces of you that feel broken and addressing them one by one. This is where having your therapist on board can be helpful, they can listen and provide you with professional support when addressing the particularly painful parts that you have been holding on

168

to. You can also use other practices, such as yoga or spirituality, to draw you into yourself and help you explore the parts of yourself that have been hurt and hidden for a long time.

Shifting your focus is another essential part of healing from abuse. You need to make sure that you are engaging in your reality and focusing on the world around you. Be patient with yourself and practice engaging bit by bit. This is a good time to practice rebuilding your independence, going out on your own and with loved ones without the abuser, and being your true-self. The parts of you that were dormant for so long can now be appreciated and adored again. Ask people how they are doing, get involved in the lives of the ones you love, and begin integrating yourself with the world around you again.

It is time to start bathing in self-love again.

Chapter 9: Healing Your Sense of Self

In Chapter 8 we discovered the importance of various healing strategies that would protect you from the physical and neurological aspects of your abuse. However, there are many psychological aspects that you are going to need to heal as well. Being able to reintegrate into society after having been a victim of narcissistic abuse is extremely challenging. As a result of your abuse, many aspects of your life have become casualties. You have more than likely lost many friends and family members, hobbies and passions, your sense of self-worth and self-image, your self-respect, and other important aspects of your life. If you truly want to heal all the way from your narcissistic relationship and the damage you have endured, you need to focus on healing these aspects of your life as well. In this chapter, we are going to explore how you can do just that.

Restoring Your Sense of Self

After an abusive relationship, losing your sense of identity is an extremely common, yet extremely damaging side-effect. This is exactly what results in victims staying in abusive relationships for so long, and why relapses occur. The victim simply does not recognize themselves outside of the relationship anymore. Rebuilding your sense of self after leaving your narcissistic relationship is a vital step in healing yourself so that you can begin living again. This is how you can begin to remember who you are, rebuild your confidence, self-respect and self-esteem, and feel worthy of being a part of society once more.

The first step to doing this is to focus on remembering that you are worthy. It can take some time to rebuild your sense of self-worth. You can begin healing your sense of self-worth by affirming it to yourself on a regular basis. In the mirror each morning, focus on affirming your worth to yourself. Affirmations like "I am worthy," "I deserve to be happy and healthy," and "I deserve to be respected" are great affirmations to begin building your sense of self-worth. You can also begin affirming yourself any time you make decisions. If you do not feel comfortable affirming in front of the mirror, you can write down positive affirmations that resonate with you in a journal. Or you can listen to a positive affirmation's audiobook. Whatever you are comfortable with. Creating these affirmations for yourself is a powerful way of personally reminding yourself that you do, in fact, deserve to be happy, healthy, respected, and loved. This will slowly begin to unwire all that was built-up on the contrary by your abuser.

Next, you need to begin rebuilding your support team. Being able to feel worthy and deserving of a great life will require you to have those feelings reinforced by others. Here, you are not looking for someone else to affirm to you what you cannot affirm in yourself. That would be a byproduct of codependency as opposed to a healthy support system. Instead, look for supportive people who can help you affirm these things to yourself. People who are willing to help you see this in yourself can support you in remembering during your more challenging times that you deserve to heal and have a better life. You want to surround yourself with good energy and a supportive environment.

You can also begin building your confidence by building your knowledge. One of the first ways that you should do this when you are healing from an abusive relationship is to begin building your knowledge in the abuse that you endured (in this case, narcissistic abuse,) and the symptoms you have as a result. Understanding this can empower you to see where you were lured in and how it was not your fault. It can also help you feel more confident in refraining from being trapped in another similar situation in the future. When you can begin to identify and understand the warning signs, it becomes a lot easier to feel confident in your own ability to protect yourself and support yourself in having better experiences in the future when you are ready.

Lastly, make sure that you spend time getting to know your *own* warning signs and symptoms. Pay attention to what it feels like to dislike something and how it feels to choose in your favor. Begin listening to your inner voice again and trusting in it. After the abuse, trusting yourself on even the most basic things can be a challenge. Letting yourself remember what this voice sounds like and trusting in it, is a big way of giving your power back to yourself so that you can become your own advocate once again.

Spending Time Doing What You Love

For as long as you have been in the relationship with the narcissist, you have likely never been allowed to have time to engage in doing what you love. If you did, it was likely heavily conditioned and controlled by your narcissistic partner. As a result, you may feel many emotions of shame, guilt, and uncertainty around doing the things that you love doing. However, it is essential that you begin. Giving yourself the time to build up to doing what you love again can support you in feeling worthy, but it can also support you in having greater confidence in actually engaging in these activities.

When you first start doing what you love again, you may feel many emotions arise within you. Of these emotions might include deep feelings of unworthiness that result in you feeling like you no longer want to engage in these activities anymore. It is important that you address where these emotions are coming from. If you feel like you personally do not want to do these activities anymore, there may be a good chance that it is because of the trauma bond and your CPTSD. To see if this is genuinely your own dislike or as a result of your conditioning, commit to doing the things that you used to love doing for a set amount of time and ensure that you continue going for the entire duration that you decided early on. Then, at the end of that period, revisit your commitment. If you decide you still do not like doing that activity anymore see if you can replace it with a new one.

If you find that you are struggling to derive any joy at all from any of the activities you try, make sure that you bring this up with your therapist. One big symptom of CPTSD derived from abuse is depression, which can result in you feeling like nothing brings you joy anymore. In this case, there may be alternative solutions to help you overcome this sadness so that you can get back to doing the things you love.

Do not feel the need to do everything you love all at once. Take your time and start with just two things. One can be bigger, like an activity or hobby that you love, and one can be smaller, like indulging in the tea that you love or adding a small element back into the daily routine that brings you joy. Having these two easy commitments to start off with will give you time to settle back into doing things you love without feeling overwhelmed. Then, as you begin to feel more confident and comfortable with these activities, you can add in more until you are doing all of the things you love once again. If you ever begin to feel overwhelmed with what is on your plate, know that you are in control and you are allowed to slow down and adjust as needed. Stay focused and clear on what your needs are and make sure that you continue to address them as you go. When you were in the abusive relationship, your needs were rarely met or addressed. For that reason, overlooking them can lead to anxiety and stress. However, having more attention on them than you are used to can do the same. Taking it easy and letting yourself have space and time needed to readjust is important.

Focusing on Your Exercise and Diet

When we are under a certain amount of stress in our lives, the first things we tend to overlook are our exercise needs and our diets. Neglecting these is a sign that you are under a lot of stress, but they are also common when we stop addressing our own needs in favor of another person's, such as in an abusive relationship. When you are reintegrating after a significant relationship that was ridden with abuse, it is important that you place emphasis on your exercise needs and your diet. Getting the right amount of nutrition and exercise can do you a world of wonders in supporting your body and mind in having the proper nutrients to lift it out of chronic stress and alleviate the symptoms that come with chronic stress.

For your exercise needs, it is a good idea to consider joining some form of exercise class or a group with others who will exercise with you. This can support you in staying dedicated, as well as support you in relearning how to socialize outside of your abusive relationship. Creating new friendships, contacts, and individuals can be refreshing. These individuals do not know your ex-partner, so they are not likely to have any idea of what your ex-partner may be spreading about you through smear campaigns. Additionally, they do not know you as an "abused person," meaning that you are free to just be *you* around them. This freedom, alongside a healthy new exercise regimen, can be very helpful to anyone who is coming back from an abusive relationship.

You should also make sure that you are eating properly. Those in abusive relationships have a tendency to either under eat or overeat due to stress. Depending on which you struggle with, you will need to choose a healthy diet plan to help you eat a healthy, balanced diet that is appropriate for your needs.

There are also some nutrients that you can use to help you with your mood when you are healing from the mental and emotional side effects of abuse. Vitamins B and D, niacin, and omega fatty acids are all known to help promote greater brain health and elevate moods. Adding these to your diet can support you in having better health overall so that you can begin enjoying your healing process and finding more joy in your day to day life.

Rebuilding Relationships That You Lost

Over the course of an abusive relationship, many other relationships are lost. As a way to prevent you from being able to see the capacity of what you are trapped in, and to avoid you leaving, abusers will always do their best to isolate you from anyone you were previously close with. Furthermore, the shame, embarrassment, trauma bond, co-dependency, and CPTSD you experience as a result of your abusive relationship can lead to you isolating yourself as well. This means that over even a relatively short period of time with a narcissist you can lose a lot of relationships with members of your family and your friends.

As you heal from the narcissistic relationship, rebuilding these relationships is important. Each of these relationships represents something you lost during the relationship with the narcissistic partner, so healing them can help you heal in general. However, going about healing these relationships may be uncomfortable or even difficult. Knowing how to repair something that has been so deeply damaged can be a struggle for people who are already going through so much as a result of the aftermath of an abusive relationship. For each relationship you want to repair, you may find that you feel embarrassed to approach the individual. If you isolated yourself from the relationship, you might feel guilty for doing so and worry that they will not forgive you. It is important to understand that in most cases, they will. If they don't, it is simply because they do not understand. Having a therapist to speak with as you rebuild these relationships can support you in navigating the relationship either way.

When you go into rebuilding these relationships, it is important that you are open and honest about the abuse you endured and how it impacted your life. You might worry that people will not believe you or that they will blame you for not knowing sooner and doing better. In some cases, this may happen. However, most people are actually understanding and empathetic toward these situations and will be willing to both listen to you and forgive you for the loss of contact for however long you experienced it.

After you have been open and honest, begin making an effort to communicate with these individuals on a regular basis. Rebuilding the relationship will take time and practice, so be patient and do not expect them to all get better at once. A great way to go about this part of the rebuilding is to set a goal to communicate with one person outside of your household on a daily basis. This way, you can begin rebuilding these relationships steadily but not in such a way that it becomes overwhelming and depletes your already low energy.

Ultimately, it is important for you to start hanging around positive and encouraging people for your health and well-being. This will help your mind to stop replaying all the events that occurred with the narcissist and also help in preventing a relapse. It is time to start focusing on you and your life now.

Starting A New Hobby

Hobbies are a wonderful way to support your healing journey. They are great for distracting you from what you have experienced, offering you a boost of confidence by giving you a sense of understanding and knowledge over something you enjoy, connect you with other people who share the same hobby and support you in networking, and promote a sense of happiness and joy within you. There are many positive benefits to having a hobby that you can enjoy in your life.

The key when healing from an abusive relationship that encouraged self-isolation is to choose a hobby that is going to support you in getting together with other people. If you enjoy something that tends to be more solitary, such as reading, consider joining a book club that will allow you to get together with others and begin socializing in a normal setting again. This way, you can do your hobby on your own time but also gain the valuable benefits of socializing out of it.

The hobbies that you choose to get into once again can be new or ones that you loved previously. There is no limit on which you can choose or how many. This is a great time to practice listening to your inner desires and needs and doing something you love. Choosing something that you are interested in and that will bring you great joy is a wonderful way to remind yourself that you are worthy of having joy and love in your life and that happiness is something you deserve to experience. This could include playing a musical instrument you have always wanted to learn how to play, or perhaps taking up a new sport or maybe learning to speak a new language. This is a great way to practice self-love and begin adding things back into your life that makes you happy. It is also a great way to open yourself up to new possible opportunities.

As with the other practices, when you are just starting your healing journey, focus on picking something that will be more manageable for you. Attempting to do too much at once or trying to get right back to where you were before the abusive relationship can be overwhelming and intimidating. When you realize that you are not the same person that you were before the relationship and that your ability to do things the way you once did have changed, you may actually end up feeling worse off. Starting off smaller and slower can support you in easing back into being a person with confidence, high self-esteem, and self-respect. Set manageable and reasonable goals for yourself, celebrate yourself each time you achieve them, then move on to the next one. This will make your healing journey much easier.

Physical Healing Practices
There are many powerful physical healing practices that you can begin incorporating into your regular life that can support you in healing from

abuse. Acupuncture, eye movement desensitization and reprocessing, yoga, reiki, shaman work, energy healing, and even hypnosis can be powerful in helping individuals who are healing from the aftermath of abusive relationships.

Acupuncture helps by supporting energy in moving through meridians in the body, helping to release blockages and eliminate stress build-ups. When healing from an abusive relationship, this can support you in letting go of things that you have been subconsciously holding onto for the duration of the relationship. It can also promote healing by supporting you in moving through the natural energies and emotions that come with your experience.

Eye movement desensitization and reprocessing is a practice that some therapists use that have individuals move their eyes in a specific way when recalling memories. This movement is believed to support the brain in becoming desensitized to the neural pathways that are integrated with the trauma of the abuse. It also supports you in creating new neural pathways that are healthier and that bring less stress into your body and mind.

Yoga is another wonderful exercise-based practice that you can use that supports healing. This is a form of exercise, but it emphasizes intentional movement and the processing of energy and emotions. When used regularly, it can support you in having a healthier response to stress stimuli which can support you in healing from the chronic stress you accumulate when you are in a toxic relationship with someone who is abusive, such as a narcissist.

Reiki and other energy healing practices can be powerful in supporting individuals in healing from narcissistic relationships. These practices are believed to promote the movement of energy in a way that is similar to acupuncture, but that does not use needles or, in many cases, physical touch in any way to promote this flow. Having Reiki or any other energy healing incorporated into your healing can be a great way to support you in feeling better on an emotional level.

Hypnosis is another type of healing, sometimes associated with energy healing, that can support you in releasing trauma. When you work alongside a professionally trained hypnotherapist, they can tailor hypnosis sessions specifically for your needs. These sessions are designed to promote the reprogramming of new neural pathways in your brain to support healthier responses to stimuli in your environment.

Using any number of these healing strategies is a great way to support your healing overall. You can also mix them together to increase your healing capacity. The best way to discover which will work best for you is to begin practicing each one and see which feels best. Incorporate the ones that feel best into your regular healing practices. While these will not replace the support of a high-quality trauma-informed therapist and a support team, they will add to your healing and help you to heal in a whole way. Approaching your healing with a mind-body-spirit approach can ensure that you release any remnants of the trauma so that you can restore your entire self.

Crystals That Support Healing
In addition to using energy healing practices as mentioned in the previous section, there are many crystals you can add to your healing practices. Crystal therapy is believed to support individuals by adding vibrational frequencies into your energy field that promote healing. You can incorporate crystal therapy into your daily life by purchasing crystals that you can wear, hold, or keep nearby.

The following crystals are known to be great for promoting healing:
- *Rhodonite* is a crystal that is associated with the heart and is believed to support individuals in healing from a broken heart
- *Obsidian* is known to expel negative energies from your body, mind, and environment
- *Jade* is known to support you in calming your emotions and overcoming stress
- *Amethyst* can protect your energy field from psychic attacks while also supporting you in overcoming addictions (such as the

ones you have to the narcissist's "idealization" phase,) as well as to overcome depression related to your trauma

- *Banded Agate* is believed to protect you from intrusive memories, which can support you in refraining from going back to the "good" times with the narcissist
- *Sugilite* which can support you in overcoming stress related to your trauma
- *Citrine* which can help you repair your negative self-image
- *Selenite* which can help you overcome the anger associated with your trauma
- *Rose Quartz* which can promote gentle healing of the heart and bring calming love back into your life

Start Traveling

Traveling is one of the greatest things you can do for your healing and your road to recovery. While you may not want to start traveling right away, once you begin feeling better you should embark on at least one traveling journey. Traveling on your own can be a powerful way to rebuild your self-confidence and self-esteem, refresh your mind, add new experiences and practice becoming independent so that you can begin breaking your co-dependency and engage in some genuine self-care.

Many people who have survived abuse find that even when they are away from their abusive relationship, their environment is filled with memories. You may find frequent places that you went to with the narcissist, such as shopping malls, grocery stores, or other places, which bring up memories. Leaving this behind, even if only for a short period of time, can liberate you from these memories and help you gain perspective.

Plus, traveling independently gives you free time to be with yourself, remember who you are, and begin learning how to love yourself once more. You can discover how you feel best supported, what acts of self-love make you feel best, what you like to do when you are alone, and what you don't like to do. These intimate pieces of information that you gain about yourself build your self-confidence by giving you the opportunity to know yourself in a deeper way than you have for some time.

Before you embark on traveling alone, make sure that you are safe from the hoovering narcissist. Do your absolute best to make sure the narcissist does not find about your travel plans. Make sure they are blocked on your mobile-phone and blocked on every social media platform. That way, your experience remains positive, and you can focus completely on your healing and recovery.

Chapter 10: Terminology Index

Here is a list of some terminology that you may not fully understand or know the meaning of:

Accuse
When the narcissist accuses other people of engaging in destructive or abusive behaviors, such as lying, manipulating, rather than admitting that they were to blame.

Cognitive Dissonance
When it comes to psychology, cognitive dissonance means you are in mental discomfort due to holding two or more contradictory values, beliefs, or ideas. In this case, it is from trying to hold two contradictory realities together in your mind: the true reality, and the narcissistic falsehood reality.

Conditioning
The process of psychologically training or altering someone so that they behave in a desired manner.

Devaluation
The phase in the abuse cycle where your abuser attempts to reduce or eliminate your worth and importance.

Discard
The phase in the abuse cycle where your abuser attempts to discard you by withdrawing and psychologically pressuring you into a desperate attempt of "winning them back."

Gaslighting
An abuse tool where abusers invalidate the victim, manipulating them into questioning their own sanity.

Hoovering
The phase in the abuse cycle where your abuser attempts to "suck" you back in through luring you to re-engage in your relationship with them.

Love Bombing/Grooming/Idealization

When a narcissist creates a mask, appearing to be the perfect "Prince Charming" for you. Here, they put you on a pedestal and give you everything you ever wanted so that you have the illusion that you are perfect together.

Triangulation

When a narcissist brings a third party into the dynamic of your relationship to use against you. The third person is awarded attention, affection, and respect while you are neglected and abused.

Narcissistic Supply

The people who have already been abused by the narcissist and are more likely to come back. These are people who are most vulnerable to being readmitted into the abuse cycle with the narcissist, feeding their needs. A narcissist regularly keeps a few on hand in case they are not being fueled elsewhere.

Projection

When an individual project's their beliefs, values, opinions, emotions, actions, or behaviors onto another person. In a narcissistic relationship, this is where the abuser would blame the victim for something that was actually done by the abuser.

Smear Campaign

When an abuser discredits you to friends, family, and anyone who may be capable of supporting or assisting you behind your back. This is how they gain power by eliminating your validation and credibility and leading others to believe the narcissist over you.

Stonewalling

When a narcissist or abuser becomes evasive and begins blocking or delaying you. They will regularly give vague or evasive answers to questions or simply ignore you until they feel like stopping.

Reality Distortion

When an individual alters another's reality for their own personal gain. For the narcissist, they alter their victims' sense of reality through evil tactics such as compulsive lying, manipulation, and victimization.

Victimization

When someone turns themselves into the victim, even though they are not necessarily the victim of the circumstances. In narcissistic relationships, this is a manipulation tactic used by the narcissist to cause the victim to feel as though the narcissist is the true victim, thus causing the narcissist's victim to feel guilty and remorseful. In this case, the victim was never in the wrong, to begin with, but the narcissist has expertly flipped the switch and caused them to feel like they were.

Final Words

Thank you for reading *"Emotional and Narcissistic Abuse: The Complete Survival Guide to Understanding Narcissism, Escaping the Narcissist in a Toxic Relationship Forever, and Your Road to Recovery."*

I recognize that based on the nature of this book, it can be a challenging one to read. You may be facing many emotions after reading it, so I hope you have been seeking support or finding ways to allow yourself to integrate this information so that you can use it to support your escape and healing processes.

If you have already left the narcissistic relationship, I commend you. I know that is a very challenging process and you have done a wonderful thing. If you are struggling, be sure to reach out for help and continue reaching until you are pulled out. I know this can be an extremely challenging time. Do not beat yourself up over it. Trust that this is not your fault and that you are absolutely not to blame for any of this, no matter what anyone may try and tell you. There is a happily ever after for you.

The next step is to carry on in healing from the breaking or now-broken bond between you and your abuser. Continue working in the direction of healing as much as you can, taking it one step at a time and always focusing on the outcome. Trust that you have an outcome on the way and that it will not always be like this.

It is natural to feel stuck or unable to do this on your own. That is because healing from abuse is a painful process that often requires professional support and a lot of time and effort put into healing. Please do make sure that you reach out. I know that until now you have been conditioned to isolate yourself. This should be the first thing you start undoing by reaching out and receiving support from others. Keep trying until you get it; you can do this. Even if it has been some time since you left and you are feeling stuck, reach out. There is no time frame for healing. Do what you need to do. Be kind and be patient with yourself.

It is important to note that many people who experience narcissistic abuse during a toxic relationship with a narcissist are likely to be particularly sensitive and can easily feel the emotions and feelings of others. If this sounds like you, there is a good chance you are an Empath. If you don't know what an Empath is or you are curious to find out more, be sure to check out my other book *"Highly Sensitive Empaths: The Complete Survival Guide to Self-Discovery, Protection from Narcissists and Energy Vampires, and Developing the Empath Gift."*. In it, you can learn more about what being an Empath means, how it impacts you, why narcissists are drawn to you, and how you can protect yourself on a deeper, energetic level.

Lastly, if you found this in any way helpful to you, please take the time to review it on Amazon. Your honest feedback would be greatly appreciated and it will greatly help many other lost souls out there who may be struggling and in a time of need.

Thank you.

Made in the USA
Lexington, KY
04 June 2019